PENG

THE PRICE OF ONIONS

Ashok V. Desai, who is currently a visiting scholar at Stanford University, is best known for his columns in *Business Standard*, of which he is consultant editor, and in *BusinessWorld*; they demystify current economic issues with lucidity and wit. Earlier he served as chief consultant in the finance ministry from 1991 till 1993, when he helped Manmohan Singh with the reforms. His reflections on the reforms led to his last book, *My Economic Affair*. Desai's first book, *Real Wages in Germany 1871-1913* is still cited as a standard reference work on German economic history. Although he leaves his heart in India, Desai has ranged far: he studied economics in Cambridge, taught in Oxford, Bombay, Delhi and Suva (Fiji), did research in Berlin and Brighton, and ran an energy project in Ottawa. He enjoys eating and drinking in the company of friends.

PENGUIN BOOKS

ASHOK V. DESAI

The Price of Onions

PENGUIN BOOKS

Penguin Books India (P) Ltd., 11 Community Centre, Panchsheel Park, New Delhi 110 017, India
Penguin Books Ltd., 27 Wrights Lane, London W8 5TZ, UK
Penguin Putnam Inc., 375 Hudson Street, New York, NY 10014, USA
Penguin Books Australia Ltd., Ringwood, Victoria, Australia
Penguin Books Canada Ltd., 10 Alcorn Avenue, Suite 300, Toronto, Ontario, MAV 3B2, Canada
Penguin Books (NZ) Ltd., Cnr Rosedale and Airborne Roads, Albany, Auckland, New Zealand

First published by Penguin Books India 1999

10 9 8 7 6 5 4 3 2 1

Typeset in *Nebraska* by SÜRYA, New Delhi
Printed at Chaman Enterprises, New Delhi

For Ena

Contents

Introduction

Economics afflicts us all. A father may worry about how he is going to find the dowry for his daughter by the time she is to marry: he faces an intertemporal budget constraint. The mother may wonder how she is going to get the daughter ready for school and finish cooking for her husband by the time she has to leave for work: she has a time allocation problem. The daughter may count her pocket money and puzzle over how she can buy a birthday present to take to her friend's party this evening: she faces a liquidity problem. They all face economic problems.

It may well happen that the father wins a lottery, the mother opens a restaurant that does not open till noon, and the daughter becomes a software engineer and earns enough to buy ten husbands. If their lives turn out so happily, they will attribute the turn of events to good luck; but their good fortune is as economic an event as their sufferings. Economics is a strictly neutral subject; it makes people happy as often as sorry. It offers solutions as often as it poses problems.

But it would be impossible to find an economist who will cheer you up. Economists pretend to be like doctors: they claim to have cures for the ills of an economy, and formulae to help people earn more and work less. But no one can drop into an economist's clinic and buy a magic formula. For economists, like us common mortals, are slaves of the market. So they teach in colleges, write multicoloured reports for bankers, or grey papers for the government. They too have household budgets to balance, mistresses to please, old age to provide for. They sell their services wherever they get the best price. It is not in their agenda to make something for ordinary humans, nor does it occur to humans that economists could be of any earthly use.

I too was once a normal economist. I did market surveys for women's underwear, forecast demand for steel wire, advised developing countries on how to cope with the oil crisis. I wrote papers that would take me to conferences in exotic resorts. I found economics useful for making a living. I hoped it was useful to those who paid for my work; but the thought that it may be relevant to the common man did not really strike me. Then, just as I was getting ready to retreat into comfortable obscurity, my luck turned.

In 1987 I had just returned to India after a stint in Canada and was looking for work. I met a friend, who was then in the Planning Commission. He asked me to do him a study on trade policy. 'Never,' I said, 'You will never pay for it.' That sounds like a shocking thing to say about our sovereign government. But ever since the 1960s when I started working in this country, my views were somehow never quite what the government wanted to hear. I feared that when my friend received my study, he would hem and haw, write notes up and send memos down, but would never get approval to pay for the treasonable tract he had inspired.

Anyway, Joshi persuaded me and I started the study. It was finished two years later and went to Mr Amar Nath Verma, Member-Secretary of the Planning Commission. Just as I had feared, notes went up and down, approvals were vainly sought, but there was no sign of payment. I went to see Mr Verma. He raised one eyebrow and said, 'Yes?' I said there was this small matter of a payment. I cannot remember whether the cheque arrived, for as related below, I went on to bigger things. Later on Mr Verma went on to become Principal Secretary to the Prime Minister and Master String-puller; he also became a good friend.

While I was pleading with him for payment, however, I had sent a copy to Manmohan Singh, who was then adviser to Chandra Shekhar, the Prime Minister. Manmohan Singh has a terrible vice: he actually reads the stuff his friends give him. Worse still, he remembers it. In that study, I had suggested a way of abolishing import licences: they were extremely paper-intensive, took months to issue, created enormous corruption, and did great harm to exports. I suggested that of the export earnings, the government should buy a certain proportion at a fixed rate of exchange for its own use. Against the rest, the government should issue import replenishment certificates to the exporters—import licences which could be used to import anything. These import replenishment certificates would be issued in standard denominations—Rs 1000, Rs 1 million etc.—and exporters should be allowed to sell them if they wanted. In this way, a market in the certificates would emerge, and even those who were not exporters would be able to get imports by buying the certificates on the market. The certificates would serve both as carriers of an export subsidy and as import entitlements, without the red tape of the Chief Controller of Imports and Exports.

In the next six months, Chandra Shekhar stepped down as Prime Minister, the Congress formed the government, and Manmohan Singh became finance minister. To my surprise, the new government introduced the import replenishment certificates, which were renamed eximscrips. The experiment was a roaring success. More important, it gave the government confidence; it abolished the eximscrips in 1992, allowed exporters to sell their portion of the foreign exchange earnings in the open market, and freed industrial inputs and machinery of import licensing. In this way, an unnecessary part of controls, which vested interests in the government and business had kept alive for fifty-three years, was swept away. I claim no credit for this, for many others have, and success is allowed to have many fathers. But I was quite happy to have been one of the many. I also realized that economics could sometimes be used to improve policy.

Manmohan Singh did not stop at taking my idea; he took me into the finance ministry in 1991 to help him reform the Indian economy. By a quirk of fate I, who had spent a quarter century in futile and lucrative criticism of the government, found myself called upon to help in making policies for others to criticize.

But I found that the need of the hour was not to make policy but to cheer up the finance minister. Those were hard times; inflation was running at 15 per cent. The Reserve Bank had mortgaged its gold with the Bank of England, and was scraping the bottom of its foreign exchange reserves. Importers had to put down double the value of their imports in a bank before they were allowed to import. Oil stocks were running low, and we were haunted by possible shortages of kerosene, petrol and diesel oil. People affected by the hardships were in a foul mood; industrialists were cutting down production, and trade unions were marching workers out on the streets. Traditional socialist remedies had been tried and had failed. The businessmen, bureaucrats and politicians who benefited from the old policies resisted the trying out of new ones.

Manmohan Singh bore the brunt of this resistance. It was unpleasant and frustrating, and it used to depress him. One of my tasks was to take to him the weekly figure of inflation every Thursday evening. Inflation was going up, and the inflation figures were not encouraging.

So one day I decided to cheer him up. I made up a simple recursive model, and used it to predict how inflation would behave in the next few months. It said that inflation would come down below 10 per cent in six months. I drew a beautiful graph showing the forecast and took it with my usual Thursday inflation figure to Manmohan Singh.

I thought he would be delighted; but he was scandalized. 'Never do this again,' he said. 'Suppose it comes out in the press that the finance ministry was predicting a fall in inflation and it didn't come down; where will I be then?'

But I went on making forecasts. Inflation began to come down. As it came down, Manmohan Singh became less allergic to my forecasts. Then, as I had predicted, it fell below 10 per cent. After that Manmohan Singh would himself say, 'As my advisers tell me, inflation will come down further . . .' That is when I began to feel that economics could be a useful subject.

In those two years we introduced a number of reforms. Government expenditure greatly exceeded its revenue. We reduced the gap by cutting down fertilizer subsidies. We reduced income tax rates; as a result, tax evaders began to pay taxes, and tax receipts shot up. Reserve Bank of India used to fix forty-six different interest rates. We unfixed most of them, and reduced cross-subsidies from some borrowers to others; as a result, all interest rates came down. All this was achieved with teamwork; the government is a huge juggernaut, and nothing can be done without involving masses of bureaucrats.

I was, however, keen on one reform which proved difficult to achieve. The supply of industrial inputs we produced within the country was limited and could not support much further increase in exports; to export more, we had to import inputs. There was no longer any difficulty in finding foreign exchange for them; we had created a market in exchange, and it could be bought or earned by exporting. But import duties were high, and were obstructing exports produced from imported inputs. In theory, exporters could import the inputs without paying import duty; but for that they had either to get duty-free import licences in advance of exports and later satisfy the government that they had actually used the imported inputs to make the exports, or they had to pay duty and reclaim it from the government after exporting. Both these devices involved considerable corruption and delay. Thus, high import duties were the biggest obstacle to increasing exports. We had reduced the value of the rupee from 5½ cents to 3½ cents approximately. This devaluation raised the cost of imports by over 50 per cent. So there was much scope for reducing import duties.

But we could not afford to reduce the duties. For that would have caused loss of revenue. We had taken a loan from the International Monetary Fund at the height of our troubles in 1991; one of the conditions of that loan was that we would reduce the deficit in the central budget every year. The deficit reductions we were asked to make were so drastic that Manmohan Singh did not feel he could reduce import duties.

The matter came to a head when we began to make the 1993 budget. I argued that we should begin to reduce import duties. Apart from the need to stimulate exports, industry was in doldrums and a tax cut would help it to revive. A colleague argued that the IMF's standby loan came to an end that year and that we would need another; in the circumstances we could not afford to disregard the IMF's requirements. I made a forecast: I said that the foreign exchange reserves would go up by at least $4 billion the following winter, and that we would not need another IMF loan. My colleague thought it was too hazardous to rely on my astrology.

Manmohan Singh thought about our arguments for two days, and finally decided to accept my advice. That is how we began the reduction in import duties which led to the magnificent export boom of 1993-96. But with that triumph, I dug my grave. My colleague proceeded in the next months to take away my powers, and cut me out of the information flows within the ministry. When I complained to Manmohan Singh, he said, 'You'd better get on with him; he is worth his weight in gold to me.'

When I lost my role in policy-making, I asked Manmohan Singh what he wanted me to do; he asked me to write policy briefs for him. The briefs I wrote were later published in *My Economic Affair* (New Age Publishers, Delhi, 1994); they describe what was wrong with our policies then and how it could be corrected. Most of it still remains wrong, for after 1993, Manmohan Singh's ability to push through reforms decayed. For the foreign exchange reserves went up as I had predicted, and once the balance of payments was out of the woods, the politicians did not need Manmohan Singh.

Nor did he need me, for I was only interested in changing things, not in running them. Late on the night of 30 September 1993, I erased my files on the computer, left North Block, picked up a suitcase from my home, and flew to Berlin. It was a week before the press found out; by then I was no longer around to answer their questions. Thus I avoided embarrassing Manmohan Singh.

Although my career in the finance ministry came to an untimely end, I am grateful to Manmohan Singh for one thing: he convinced me that economics mattered—that it really determined the destiny of nations. Even more, he showed me that economics works—that it really describes in fairly reliable terms the likely consequences of events and policies. This conviction is implicit to economists; when they write textbooks or learned papers, they assume without question that they are talking about the real world. But my teachers, Nicholas Kaldor and Joan Robinson, had brought me up on scepticism about mainstream economic theory, and I retained throughout a feeling that economics was a bit of a game—that it was not quite real. Now I know that it is real all right. It is not carved in stone; the economics one finds in learned journals and books is not gospel. It still has to be discovered, to be puzzled over. But there is something there to be discovered. And the way one discovers it is by applying it to real-world phenomena.

Once, when he was pained by a mechanically neoclassical essay I had written, Kaldor said to me, 'The point of doing economics is to improve one's judgement of public affairs.' That is what I try, week after week, in my columns in *Business Standard* and *BusinessWorld*. Those columns have faithful readers; their critical interest gives me much pleasure.

But public affairs are ephemeral, and so is my commentary on them. In this book I would like to take up some economic phenomena that concern readers all the time—phenomena which underlie public affairs. I first take up prices, which are a matter of worry to all of us consumers at least some of the time. I then go on to something just as familiar if not so talked about, namely consumption, and its measure, the standard of living.

Then I go on to production, which is somewhat more abstruse, and show the bits that make up the jigsaw puzzle of the production system. Finally, I take up the most difficult area of economics, namely economic policy. Most economists aspire to shape policy, but all who have done so know what a strange animal the government is, how small a part of policy relates to economic policy, and how little we know how an economy would behave at any time.

This book was more than half written when the Chernobyl virus entered my laptop through the internet and wiped off the hard disk on 26 April. Just then, four students of Delhi School of Economics—Udit Bhatia, Ratika Narag, Kartikeya Singh and Aparajita Zutsi—walked into my room and asked me to give them work. They reconstructed the destroyed graphs and tables. It was clever of them to drop in on me. They are so good that I hope they will drop by one day and write my books.

This book is not meant to educate or instruct; for those who wish to learn economics, there are many excellent textbooks. It aims to make an aimless exploration. I think that a smattering of economics enables one to see quite ordinary events in a more interesting light; that is what I would like to show. It is a bit like scuba diving; seascapes look very different, more brilliant and colourful, if one dives with a mask than if one watches them from a boat. Economics helps one bring out the hidden meaning of day-to-day phenomena. If I can show this in a lighthearted way, without being preachy or ponderous, if you feel like reading it at one go, I shall feel that I have accomplished my mission.

New Delhi **Ashok V. Desai**
September 1999

I

The Dance of Prices

I knew a man who could not bear to look at a mountain range; it reminded him of a price chart and the fortune he had lost in speculation on stock prices. We may not be quite so stricken, but the economic artefact that we run into most often is prices. It is usually the prices of things of daily use that bother us most. Prices determine how much we spend; our expenses keep bumping against the money we have, and if we cannot manage within our means, the bumps can be quite painful. As people get older, they usually get richer. But even then, most never become so comfortable that they do not have to look at the right side of the menu. They can only inure themselves to the pain of doing without.

But never quite. People still get upset when the balance between income and outgo that they have carefully devised is upset by a sudden rise in prices. It is easy to think that some evil power must be behind the rise. There may be. If the price of kerosene goes up, you know who is behind it: the government. But all prices are not raised by evil powers. Usually it is possible to guess what is happening. But a number of guesses are possible; the difficulty comes in deciding which guess is right. And if you are trying to make a policy to reduce price rise, it becomes important to make the right guess.

ONIONS

In the summer of 1998, the price of onions rose sharply. Onions are the classic poor man's food. When I was a child, a poor farm worker going to the field was apt to carry bajri ki roti, gur and onions. Even if he cooked potatoes or vegetables, onions were likely to be a part of the sabzi. Even in our own times, a Punjabi lunch would be incomplete without a salad made of raw tomatoes, onions and turnips; I remember my sense of deprivation when, on my way to Kasauli last summer, I ate in wayside restaurants and they served salads without onions. People elsewhere are not so fond of raw onions; they are positively unfashionable among the nice-smelling people. But in most parts of India, onions would be added to at least one dish for taste, and might be put into a raita. That is why the rise in the price of onions caused such a hue and cry.

The price of onions is volatile, as figure 1 shows. The prices shown are annual averages; these are smaller than within-the-year variations. But even then, near-doubling of prices from one year to the next is not unusual; and price cycles are very short. It is almost as if a rise one year will be followed by a fall next year.

One cause of the rise in onion prices was well known—the onion crop was smaller. But the crop was only about 15 per cent less than normal; how could it explain a tenfold rise in the price, from the usual Rs 6 to Rs 60 a kilogram?

That bit is easy to explain; all one has to do is to draw a graph like the one below (figure 2). What a price does is to ration out what is available to those who would buy it. Buyers can be found for a crop of 25 million tons at Rs 6 a kilogram. If the crop falls to 21 million tons, it will be

Fig 1. Price index of onions divided by wholesale price index

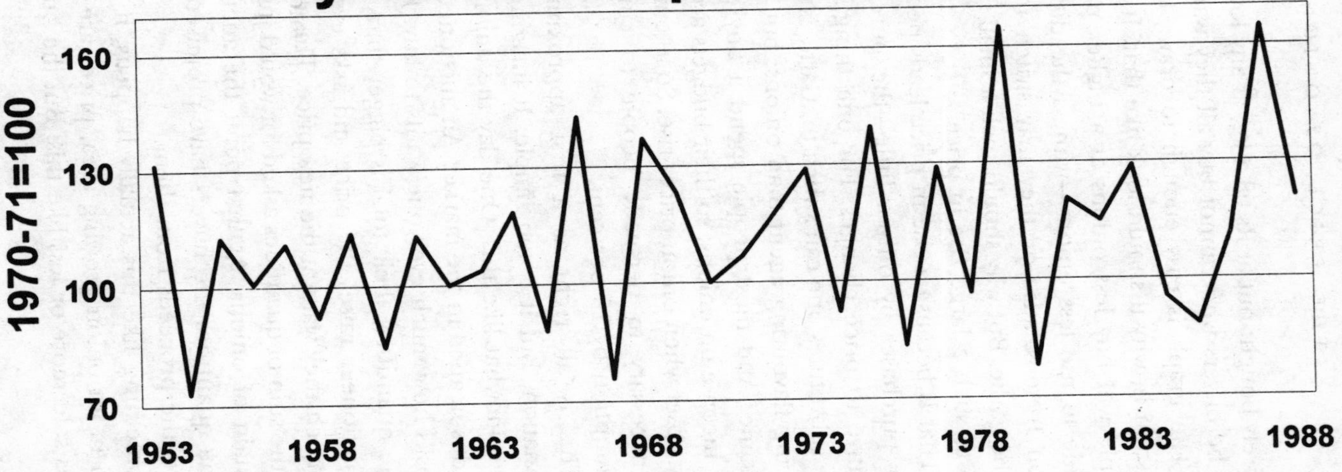

entirely bought out at Rs 68 a kg; at any lower price there will be buyers who cannot buy all they want.

The graph is easy enough to draw. The interesting question is, why it should look like that. It is obvious that people will buy less onions at a higher price: they may decide to use less onions—witness the disappearance of onion from salads—or they may switch to a substitute: maybe garlic. But why should such a small fall in the crop lead to such a large rise in price?

That is because a rise in price leads people to reduce their purchases by only a little—the purchases are not sensitive to price changes. For one thing, there are no close substitutes one can switch to. Garlic is an even more enticing flavouring agent than onions; but it is not quite the same. And most people spend a tiny proportion of their income on onions; so their budgets are not quite so badly upset when onion prices rise. So a tenfold price rise was necessary to persuade people to cut down their consumption by 10 per cent.

This is all right as a first approximation to an explanation. But it is too simple. It imagines that prices form somewhat like this. One day the onion crop comes in and is heaped in the market. An auctioneer sets a price and asks how much everyone wants to buy. He then adds up the quantities; their total is bigger than the crop. So the auctioneer raises the price and asks everyone to say how much they want at the new price. This ritual goes on until the sum of quantities asked for would just sell out the mountain of onions. At that point the auctioneer doles out the quantities the buyers have promised to buy and collects the proceeds from them.

Something like this actually happens; if you go to a mandi in an onion growing area, prices are formed and arrivals sold more or less like this. But the buyers are not

Fig 2. Onions bought at various prices

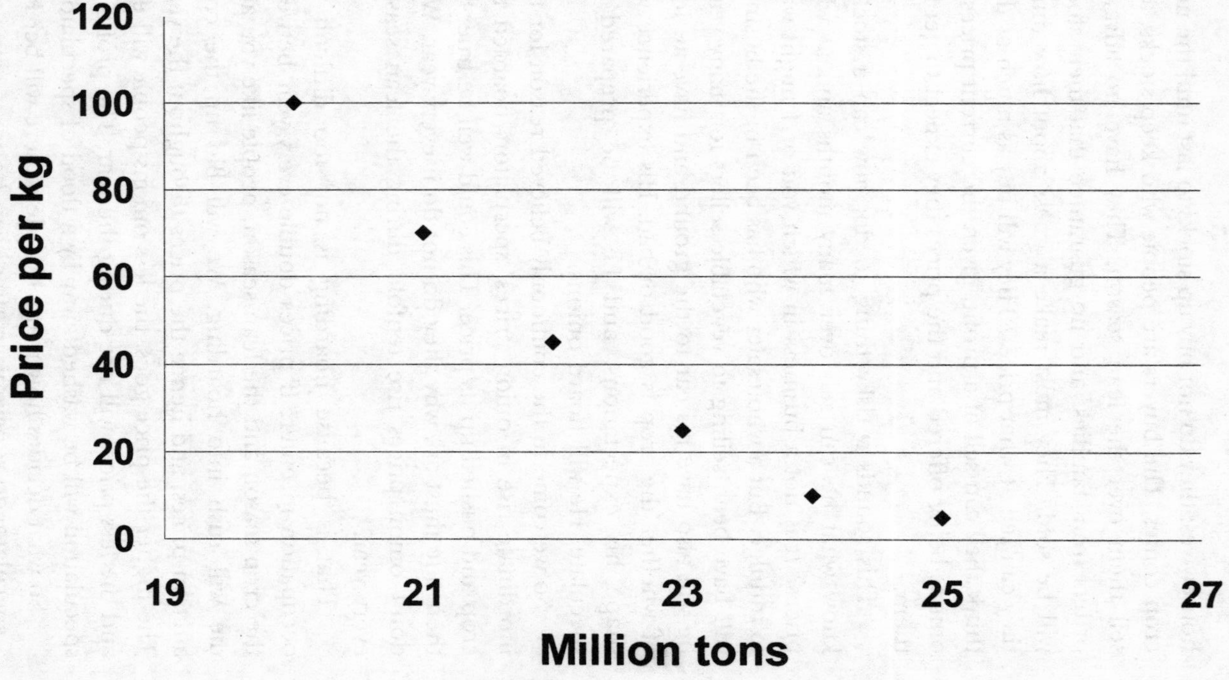

housewives; they do not buy up stocks to last until the next crop comes. The buyers are people who keep stocks, and sell them over the lean season. They have no advance orders from families, and no guarantee that their stocks will be sold. They must make a guess about how much they can sell at what prices. They will buy as much as they think they can sell at a profit, given the current prices of onions being offered and the prices they expect to get for them.

This sounds a risky thing to do; how can a stockist know what he can sell over many months and at what prices? It is not a business in which you or I might want to indulge. But a wholesaler who has been in the business will have been selling to vegetable sellers for many years; he will also have his ear to the ground and have an idea of whether the crop is good or bad. His experience will shape his expectations, and he will be prepared to speculate. He will hoard onions.

So we come to the commonly believed reason for the inordinate rise in onion prices: speculators hoarded the crop and pushed up its price. This could well be true; but then one must ask why they do not do it every year. Why don't onion prices rise tenfold during the lean season every year?

That is because hoarding is not too difficult an occupation to enter. If prices double every year between the crop season and the lean season, people like you and me will rush into hoarding. We will bid up the crop auction prices, and hence the prices throughout the year. The higher the price goes, the less onions people will eat, and the less prices will rise during the year. The profits of speculation will be washed away by a flood of speculators.

So what decides how many hoarders there will be? For a speculator to survive year after year, he must cover the cost of the money he invests in the stocks, and make at least enough profit as he would in speculating on something else. If speculators consistently make a lot more, more speculators will come in; if they make less, speculators will go off to do something else. Thus ease of entry and exit into the hoarders' profession puts a cap on their long-term earnings.

The reason why prices rose tenfold last year was not that too much was hoarded. The reason is that such a big rise is unusual—it occurs maybe once in a quarter century. Hoarders did not expect it, and hence hoarded too little. So the crop was sold at prices that were too low to bring down demand sufficiently. As the year went by, hoarders' stocks depleted drastically, and a time came when the remaining stocks were so small that they could be rationed out with only a large rise in prices.

Suppose now that you are the minister of civil supplies in the BJP government. The newspapers carry news every day of rocketing onion prices. The Congress is organizing demonstrations which draw housewives by the thousand. Coalition partners are threatening to withdraw support unless onion prices are brought down. The Prime Minister is on the phone asking you to do something fast. What would you do?

Whatever you might do, you cannot increase the output of onions till the next crop comes in. You call in the Secretary. He tells you about your secret weapon—the Essential Commodities Act. This Act gives the government power to compel traders to declare their stocks, to lay down maximum stocks that can be held, and to sequester stocks. So you can send in the police and force stockists to make a declaration of their stocks, or to sell the surplus stocks to the government. Force is essential; traders would not do these things willingly. Its effectiveness must be doubtful; some policemen may make their own private compromises with the traders, and the effectiveness of those that do not must also be imperfect.

But even without thinking of these administrative defects, the consequences must make one pause. For if these measures make traders disgorge stocks, the fall in price that brings must be temporary. As long as stocks cannot be increased, scarcity can only be relieved now by making it worse later. Supplies can only be shuffled across time, and price rise can only be reduced now by raising it later.

Similarly, if the government sequesters stocks and sells them at a low price, it will only increase the total demand by doing so. Supplies to some people can only be increased by reducing them to others. Those who get onions cheaply might also sell to those who cannot.

The only action that can make a difference is to increase supplies; and if the crop comes in only infrequently, supply can be increased between crops only by importing onions. The point of importing onions is to keep prices down; the way to do it is to import onions as cheaply as possible—not by sending a charter plane to Teheran with a Joint Secretary to escort honourable onions to Delhi, but by allowing anyone who wants to import onions from wherever he likes; it is in every trader's interest to go and get onions at a lowest price, and they will do it if only they are left free to do so.

The second thing to do is to ensure that one does not land up in a situation where one has to watch prices rising inexorably. The precaution to take is to ensure that stocks are always adequate. In other words, the way to stabilize prices is not by punishing hoarders, but by making them hoard more. The cheapest way of making them do so is to give them credit to buy stocks at low interest rates. A hoarder will not hoard stocks unless the rise in price earns him at least as much as the interest he has to pay to buy the onions; the lower the interest rate, the lower the seasonal price increase he will expect.

SUGAR

The government does not normally bother much about onion prices. With sugar, on the other hand, it is always bothered. It takes away 40 per cent of sugar production and supplies it at reduced prices through fair price shops; and it decides how much sugar the mills can sell in the open market. It requires that no new sugar mill comes up within 15 kilometres of another. Till the end of 1998 it required that anyone who wanted to set up a sugar mill or expand one had to get a licence from it. And despite all this care that goes into the management of sugar supply, sugar prices change considerably from year to year.

Figure 3 shows price volatility in sugar. Compare it with figure 1; sugar prices are not quite so volatile as onion prices. But still they vary a lot. There is no government control on sugar in Britain; but sugar is always available on supermarket shelves at more or less the same price. Why do prices in those countries remain stable without any government intervention, and why are they unstable in our country despite all the intervention?

Sugar is an interesting product. In rich countries it is a necessity, in the sense that no one would buy more sugar if it got cheaper. In India it is fast sinking from a luxury to a necessity. But there were times, in quite recent centuries, when it was so much sought after that it shaped nations and colonies.

Unlike onions, sugar has a rich history. Its name in Sanskrit literature is *sharkara*; which means that some

Fig 3. Sugar in competition with gur

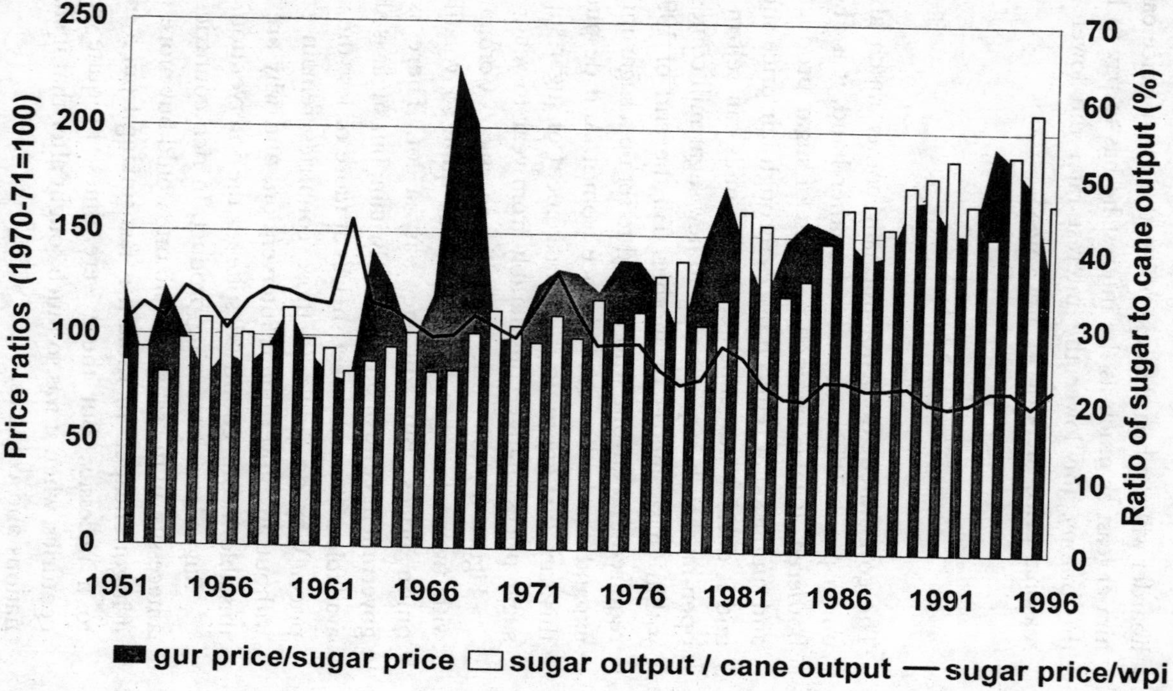

variant of it existed in India at least three thousand years ago when that word was first used. Variations of the word at least, if not the product, travelled through most of the world speaking Indo-Aryan languages, including English. But not the technology of making it; for sugar cane can only be grown in the tropics. There were substitutes, such as honey, palm gur and maple syrup. But they were not agricultural products, and their supply could not be as easily expanded as that of cane sugar. Five hundred years ago, people were probably as fond of sweets as we are, but they used a great variety of locally made sweeteners, and all were more costly than now.

Colonies and slaves

Then, beginning with the voyages of Christopher Columbus and Vasco da Gama in the 1490s, the West Europeans began to trade directly with Asia and to conquer America and Africa. As they got rich, they began to crave for more sugar. They also encountered cane-based sugar, whose supply could be easily expanded—all it needed was warm weather and lots of rain. A vast market began to open up in Europe. But Asia could not supply it. The distance and the cost were high, the ships had limited carrying capacity, and sugar had to compete for galley space with textile, which were more valuable and brought more profit. There was also the problem of paying for the imports, for the orientals did not desire European goods and had to be paid in precious metals. There were a number of products which originated in Asia but were too expensive or limited in supply—sugar, cotton and tea, for instance.

So over the sixteenth and seventeenth centuries, European adventurers worked out a solution. They collected slaves from Africa, and took them to islands or places surrounded by jungle or swamp, so that the slaves could not escape. There they set up plantations to grow sugar cane. This is how Mauritius, Jamaica, Cuba, Trinidad and Louisiana became sugar suppliers to Europe. They were settled, or 'colonized'. This was the original meaning of a colony; till fifty years ago, tropical products like sugar, coffee and tea were called 'Kolonialwaren' in Germany. Mass-produced plantation sugar was much cheaper than other sweeteners, and replaced them in the European market.

Although slavery kept the cost of labour down, it was cruel and wasteful; there were conscientious people in Britain in the eighteenth century who would not buy sugar because it was produced with slave labour. The death rate amongst slaves was dreadful; they did not reproduce themselves, and fresh slaves had to be caught in Africa and transported to the plantations in West Indies and America. Finally the British parliament outlawed slavery in 1838. Although slavery remained legal in the United States and Latin America for some time longer, Britain ruled the seas and could gradually choke off the supply of slaves.

The effects in British slave colonies were dramatic. In Jamaica, for instance, the slaves left the plantations, went off into the surrounding hills, and started fending for themselves. They were better off, but Jamaica's exports collapsed, and the nabobs who owned the plantations could no longer support mansions in London. The story was repeated in slave colony after colony; the grandees who lived in style and played politics in London were on the road to bankruptcy, and pressed the British government to save them.

That is when the British government worked out a way of replacing the slaves with indentured labourers from India. Indians were supplied to slave plantations in

Mauritius and Trinidad. The local people of Fiji were too fierce to be enslaved. So sugar plantations were started in Fiji with indentured Indian labour in the 1870s.

Indenture entailed contracts of ten to twelve years. It worked no better than slavery; labour unrest was endemic, and when workers had the choice they preferred not to renew their contracts. So gradually, indenture was replaced by tenancy farming: the plantations were divided up into plots which were leased out to the labourers, and a contract with them was made to ensure that they grew only sugar cane.

Thus sugar production was characterized by peculiar 'production relations' as Marxists call them. The Europeans, as they grew rich, asked for ever growing quantities of sugar. To ensure steady and growing supply, plantations were set up in isolated outposts on the sea that produced nothing but sugar. The huge investments in slaves, sugar mills and shipping could pay off only if the plantations were kept running without interruption. This meant a forced marriage between workers and plantations. The slaves—and later, contract workers and tenant farmers—in those plantations had no choice but to plant, grow and cut sugar cane.

Sugar in India

Sugar may well have been invented in India; but it was not sugar as we know it. It was closer to today's khandsari. If sugarcane juice is boiled, it yields gur, not the sugar of today. The juice can be filtered to give a clearer syrup and make a whiter product; the commonly used filter was bone charcoal. But however closely the syrup is purified, it will not give the modern sugar. For when it is boiled and sugar separates, some of the sugar will get burnt—'caramelized'—

and will give the product a brownish tinge. That is how khandsari is made, and why it is not as white as sugar.

This caramelization can be prevented if the syrup is boiled in a vacuum, as was discovered in the 1850s. With this, the present white or vacuum pan sugar was born. Initially this vacuum pan sugar was imported into India. But by the 1930s, sugar mills were sprouting in the cane-growing areas of north India.

However, the forced marriage between cane growers and sugar mills, which plantation owners had specially arranged in other tropical colonies, was not possible in India. Although India had supplied so many indentured labourers, India had neither slavery nor indenture; there was no way to force farmers to sell to sugar mills. Cane had competing uses: it could be used to make gur or khandsari. And because of these other claimants for cane, sugar mills had to draw cane from a large area; and remember, the typical rural roads were dirt roads, and the normal means of transport was the bullock cart.

But nationalist feeling began to grow in India from the latter years of the nineteenth century onwards; one of the nationalist themes was that the colonial government had favoured British industrialists and done too little to promote industry in India. In response to this criticism, the government began to impose duties on imports after the First World War. By the end of the 1920s, duties were almost twice as high as the price of imported sugar.

At this level of protection, sugar making suddenly took off. Sugar was the booming industry of the 1930s. Sugar mills sprouted all over north India; they took over the market from imports, and began to encroach on the market for khandsari. There was soon a glut of sugar, and millers started reducing the purchase price of cane, and became irregular in paying farmers. So in 1934 the governments of Bihar and United Provinces began to fix the minimum sale price of cane to sugar mills. Thus emerged the first element of the Indian solution to the grower–miller conflict.

With the imposition of the high tariff, imports fell rapidly. By 1937 imports were eliminated, domestic sugar mills captured the entire market, and there was such a glut that prices fell sharply. Then most of the sugar millers got together and formed a sugar syndicate to control supply to the market. Thus came the second element of the solution—cartelization of the industry.

The third element came with independence. A good deal of sugar was produced in the irrigated west Punjab, and stopped coming across after 1947. This caused a severe shortage. World production was still recovering from the ravages of the Second World War, and imports were not available. The shortage ensured that sugar had to be rationed—and the government bought it at a price it fixed. That price had to be related to the price farmers received for their cane; thus rationing involved the government in fixing the price of sugar as well as cane.

In 1956, sugar making like other industrial products came to be licensed. The Congress, which came to power after Independence, favoured cooperatives. Cooperative sugar mills were set up in irrigated areas of Maharashtra. These were very different from those of northern India. Because cooperatives were the darlings of the government, they got big loans from the governments and their financial institutions. The cooperative sugar mills were bigger, more modern and more efficient. And Maharashtra grew a different cane from northern India. North Indian cane took ten months to mature; peninsular cane took eighteen months. It yielded far more per acre, so a sugar mill could draw its supply from a smaller area. And it contained more sugar, so a sugar mill needed to crush less cane to make the same amount of sugar. And because the sugar mills were 'owned' by the farmers, there were no conflicts about payment; farmers simply took whatever was left after meeting costs and servicing loans (and often without servicing loans). The new sugar mills gave the northern ones competition that was difficult to meet. The government had to step in and protect industry in the North against competition from the southern industry.

This is how the government began to fix different prices for cane in different parts of the country. Originally the idea was simply to allow for differences in growing conditions and cane varieties. But once the central government began to fix cane prices, state governments began to press it to fix higher prices for its own farmers. Later the state governments themselves began to fix minimum cane prices that were higher than those fixed by the centre. For the politicians running state governments, cane farmers were a powerful constituency which controlled votes; sugar mills were merely important as possible sources of money.

Thus the finances of sugar mills became fragile. State governments were prone to fixing cane prices that were too high given the controlled price of sugar that the central government fixed, and sugar mills were in danger of making losses. If they got into financial trouble, they did not pay farmers their dues or delayed payment. Farmers bitten by such experience stopped growing cane the next year, and the sugar mills experienced cane shortage. This is how a cycle of surplus and shortage, high and low prices, mounting and depleting stocks emerged.

But despite these recurring crises, sugar has been taking away the market for gur. Figure 3 also shows the course of the ratio of gur price to sugar price; it is far more volatile than the sugar price. Once in three or four years sugar mills get into a financial crisis and fail to pay farmers in full. Next year farmers plant less cane. Since, in a time of shortage, gur prices can rise and the rise in sugar prices is restrained by the government, sugar production falls. But every rise in the relative price of gur diverts demand from gur to sugar. In this way, the share of cane going to sugar mills has been rising. Since 1970 this shift has been accentuated by a fall in the price of sugar relative to that of gur. Until then the government was licensing more and more small sugar mills. After 1970 some of the mills began to expand and cut costs; that slowed down the rise in the price of sugar and increased its consumption at the expense of gur.

Meanwhile, elsewhere . . .

In sugar, a large number of small farmers face a small number of sugar mills. The farmers do not want to grow anything else because sugar cane is a big yielder—yields of 80 tons a hectare are not unknown in the peninsula, and the best canefields in Hawaii yield 150 tons. They have other buyers of cane in khandsari and gur-makers; but the market for gur is limited, and khandsari is an inferior product to sugar, inefficiently made, and can survive sugar's competition only when there is a general shortage of sweeteners. Thus even though the structure of the industry is different in India—the sugar mills are smaller and the peasants are free not to grow sugar cane, the result is the same as in the classical cane areas of the world—there is a forced marriage between sugar mills and cane farmers, and two sets of governments, at the centre and in the states, play as none-too-neutral referees.

If we travelled to the original cane-growing areas of

the world—the islands and remote spots where slaves were taken to grow it—we would see a remarkable similarity between our problems and theirs. The nabobs who once used to lord it over have been replaced by companies. The slaves or indentured workers are now free farmers. But they still continue to grow cane year in year out; they continue to have quarrels with the sugar mills about the price. In some places there is a third class of cane cutters; they typically form trade unions. Thus sugar takes the typical factory culture into the countryside.

Cane cutters' unions and farmers' federations are better capable of bargaining with millers. But they are monopoly providers of labour or cane. When a monopoly seller confronts a monopoly buyer, there is often a deadlock, and the government steps in as a referee.

The difference from India is that the sugar miller is often a foreigner; sugar mills in Fiji are owned by an Australian company, and sugar mills in Jamaica by a British company. Local politicians have less control on the foreign owners. So they try and make a bargain with the governments of the countries where those owners sell their sugar. This is how the erstwhile colonies of the British empire acquired sugar quotas, first in Britain, and then in the European Economic Community (now European Union). Latin American countries similarly acquired quotas in the United States. Both the industrial trade blocks protect their markets, and impose high import duties on non-quota sugar. The Soviet Union similarly bought exclusively from Cuba; its collapse was a deadly blow for Cuba.

Thus the reason why sugar prices are so stable in industrial countries is that their governments control supply; they do not allow cheap sugar to come and compete with sugar from their ex-colonies or client countries or from their own sugar mills. They also keep up sugar prices and make their own people pay more than they would if they freely imported sugar; the people do not mind because sugar long ago became a minor necessity amongst them and high prices hurt them little. There are very few sugar companies; each owns a number of sugar mills, often in different countries. They make a good profit at the prices they get in their protected markets. They use part of the profits to keep large stocks so that there is never a shortage; this is why sugar prices are so stable in industrial countries.

Outside the industrial countries and their client countries, there is a more or less free market for sugar. Other countries also protect their own sugar mills, have their own intrigues between local politicians, millers and peasants. But together, countries outside the big sugar block markets buy a few million tons of sugar; and two countries—Thailand and Australia—have capitalized on this market. In Australia, the sugar mills own huge farms: they have reproduced the slave economies of yore, except that their workers are free to come and go. In Thailand, the farmers are big landlords who own or part-own sugar mills; there too, common ownership eliminates conflict between the peasant and the miller. The big sugar millers in these countries are focused on the international market. They look for, develop and grow new, high-yielding varieties of cane; they look for opportunities to reduce costs; they speculate in world sugar markets; they play politics when necessary. This way they keep afloat in the turbulent world sugar market. Sugar in the major exporting countries is cheap, but its price is not necessarily stable.

Stable prices or low?

If we wanted to stabilize prices in India, the solution would be simple. For the government decides how much sugar to sell each month. It fis the ration given in public distribution; the ration multiplied by the number of card holders determines how much sugar would be sold at most through ration shops. The government also decides how much sugar is sold every month in the open market. It allows sugar mills to borrow unlimited amounts from the banks to finance the unsold stocks they carry, and manipulates releases into the free market in such a way that the prices the millers get would cover the costs of interest and stock-holding. All it has to do is to fix a target price. Whenever the market price exceeds the target it should increase sugar releases; whenever the market price falls below the target it should release less sugar.

That would raise two problems. First, there is so much inflation in India that a stable price would become ridiculously low within a few years. Suppose, for instance, that prices rose at 7 per cent a year—a typical figure for India. Then they would double every ten years; if sugar price was stable, it would halve in relation to other prices every ten years. This kind of thing typically happens where politicians decide the price and the industry is owned or dominated by the government—in bus and train fares, fertilizer prices, electricity prices. If the government froze sugar prices, sugar mills would go bankrupt within a few years unless they were subsidized; the subsidies would mount every year, and would have to be paid out of the government's tax revenue. Taxpayers would then be subsidizing sugar consumers.

This is not an insurmountable problem; all one has to do is to build escalation into the price. Sugar price may be raised at 7 per cent a year—or, what comes to the same thing, 0.0185 per cent every day. If one wanted to force sugar mills to increase efficiency, one would fix the figure somewhere below 7 per cent. That is what regulators abroad do; for instance, the professor who regulates the British electricity industry allows power prices to rise at a rate equal to the rate of inflation minus a certain percentage.

But there is a more serious problem: the stocks may run out; or they may grow unmanageably large. The government cannot fix any target price and maintain it; the price has to be such that neither too much nor too little sugar would be produced at that price. Actually, the prices are fixed today so that there is no inexorable accumulation or decline of stocks: stocks rise for a few years, then they go down for a few years. But they vary enormously from year to year, and so do prices. That is what we would want to eliminate.

There are many markets in which the government has nothing to do, and where prices still do not gyrate from year to year. Take the price of detergents, or cloth. They fluctuate, but not so much as to worry people. Somehow in the markets for these commodities, the producers watch offtake, and adjust production so as to match demand. This is the natural function of producers; if sugar millers are not doing it, it is because they are not allowed to do it.

If they were to do it, they would have to be free to decide how much sugar to make, and hence how much cane to buy. Currently, state governments force sugar mills to take all the cane that comes, and regulate the milling season—the number of months sugar mills must make sugar—to adjust it to the cane available. As long as they do so, sugar output will fluctuate uncontrollably, and so will sugar prices.

Surely, though, it would not be fair if a farmer grows cane and then finds that there is no one to buy it. This must be prevented; the way to do so is to insist that sugar mills must enter into enforceable, formal forward contracts with farmers. The contract would specify the quantity of cane the farmer would supply to the mill, the date on which he would deliver it for milling, and the price he would get. The price may be a fixed one; but it could also be related to the sugar price. For instance, if sugar price is Rs 10 a kg and sugar recovery (i.e. sugar obtainable from the cane) is 10 per cent, the maximum price payable for cane would be Rs 1000 a ton (Re 1 a kg); at that price the sugar mill would earn nothing to cover its costs. The cost of cane usually comes to 60 to 70 per cent of the cost of sugar. The reference price should not be the price the mill earns, otherwise the mill will have an incentive to cheat. The price should be the price in some large market, where a mill cannot influence the price. It can be the average of prices over a period, or of prices on a number of dates—say, prices at the end of five successive months.

Thus it is not necessary for the government to have the present elaborate controls on the sugar industry. Things would work much better if, instead, the government merely insisted that both farmers and mills entered into enforceable forward contracts. It can be a simple registry of contracts which takes a deposit from both sides with each contract; whoever breaks the contract would lose his deposit, and the injured party would get it.

This is indeed how the system works in sugar-producing countries like Fiji and Mauritius. The mill issues each farmer a note at the beginning of the growing season telling him the date on which he would bring his cane to the mill. The price to be paid is based on the realized price of sugar. There are often negotiations between farmers' organizations and millers on the price to be paid, which depends on the export price. Sometimes the governments intervene in the negotiations and help them along. But no permanent controls are necessary.

FATS

Onions are a single product: or at least, all onions are recognizably similar, and a person would not feel seriously deprived if she was given a pink onion instead of a white one. Sugar and gur are both sweeteners made from the same cane; used as we are to flavourless sugar, we may mind putting gur in a cake, but if we had to we would get used to it. And if we move from one to the other, sugar cane will also be diverted from one to the other; prices chart the story of such shifts.

Fats are also imperfect substitutes like gur and sugar. But they are also produced from different ingredients coming from different parts of agriculture. Their price formation shows complications which go beyond those of onions and sweeteners.

Figure 4 shows the course of prices of some major fats consumed in India. The central one is ghee. Its price has risen more or less in line with the wholesale price over the last five decades. It can vary by 20 per cent from one year to the next; it shows peaks in years of drought—1966, 1975, 1980, 1987—or immediately following years. Its substitutes show similar volatility. The prices of all its substitutes have risen faster; the price of mustard oil has risen fastest. Of its substitutes, the price of vanaspati shows the closest variations to that of ghee; that is understandable, since vanaspati is simply imitation ghee. Other oils do not show the same time patterns.

Our affair with ghee

All fats serve the same purpose: they give cooked food a flavour that people prize. We Indians prize it more; compared to other countries, our consumption of fats per

Fig 4. Price indexes of edible fats divided by the wholesale price index

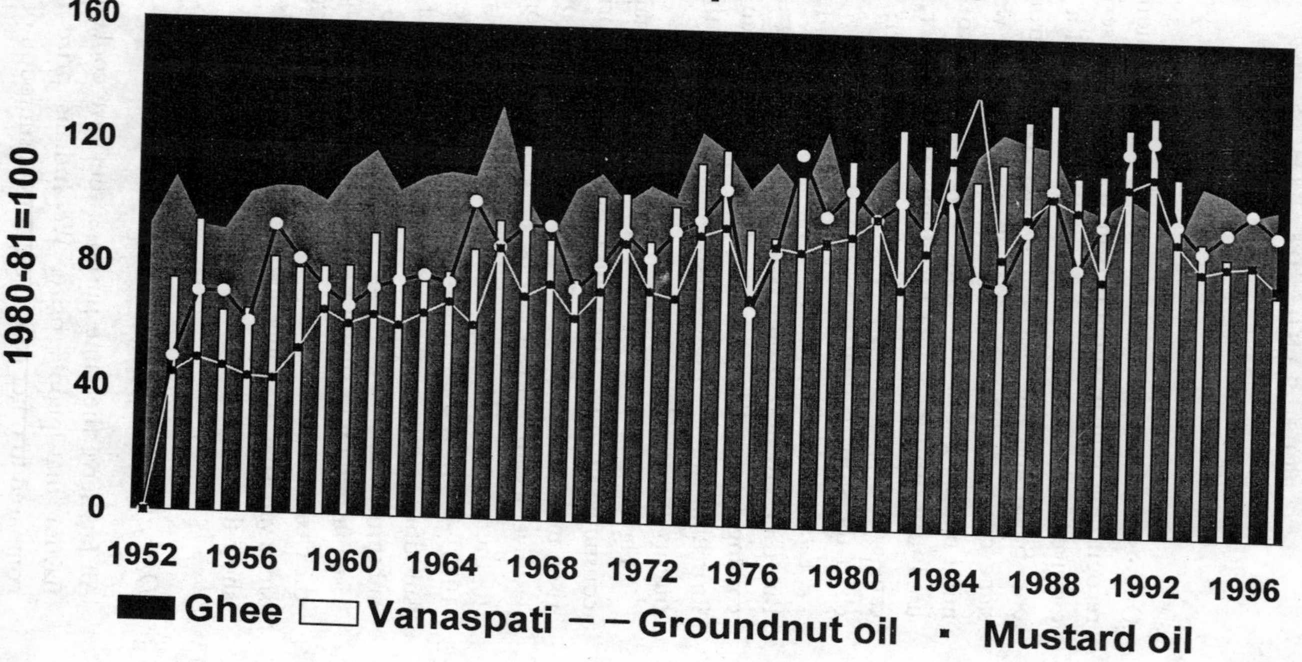

head is high. This may be because grains and vegetables are important in our diet. All animals—including ourselves—are mixtures of muscle and fat; so meat generally is cooked in its own fat. Some animals can in fact be corpulent, especially if they are fed a lot and exercised little; for instance, bacon is often more fat than meat. So meat does not need fat to cook. Nor do vegetables; but most Indians will testify that they taste much better if they are cooked with a little bit of fat—either fried or curried.

But the real reason why we like things a little fatty is probably that fats have been in our lives for millennia. Or rather, a single fat—the fat from bovine milk. It is still disputed that Aryans existed; but no one disputes that we owe much of our language and culture to them. And in their culture, two animals, the horse and the cow, played a major role. The horse was the Aryans' battle tank; cows were what they fought about, travelled with and lived on. The horse and cow—or bull—figure prominently in the myths and the scriptures of the Aryan people, wherever in the world they went; these and other cultural artefacts are the only reason to think that they existed—and that they were in India a few thousand years ago.

Properly mated, a cow gives milk; a cowherd and his family can drink as much milk as he likes—he only has to own enough cows. But milk cannot last—it has to be drunk pretty soon after it comes out of the cow. Very early therefore, the Aryan boffins worked out a way of making a more durable product out of milk, namely butter. Butter keeps fairly well at low temperatures, and was adequate for cold climates. But in India, even butter would go rancid if left out. Hence the Indians worked out an even more advanced technology, and made ghee by heating butter. This ghee can be stored for long periods; it was especially useful in India, for cows and buffaloes give more milk in winter than in summer; the excess milk produced in winter can be stored for summer in the form of ghee.

Although ghee has such a prominent place in Hindu rites and scriptures, it has to be reported with regret that all Hindus are not equally fond of it. It is most prized in the North and West—in Punjab, Rajasthan and Gujarat. In Gujarat it was invested with such magical properties that a wounded warrior was given ghee to drink. The further east and south one goes, the less people are in its thrall. They even prefer other fats for some types of cooking—the Bengalis go for mustard oil, the Maharashtrians for groundnut oil and the Telugus for sesame oil.

People vs cattle

I said earlier that a cowherd could eat ghee to his heart's content—he had to have enough cows. And he could have as many cows as he could feed. He did not have to feed them; they fed themselves. He only had to lead them to pastures. There are still nomadic tribes in Africa which wander around with hundreds of cattle, and which live on their milk, meat and blood. If there is enough land, the number of cattle a cowherd can own only depends on how many he can keep together and move around without losing.

But even the huge continent of Africa is running short of land for nomads to wander in; other continents ran out of land long ago. The number of cattle a pasture can support is strictly limited; if the number exceeds the carrying capacity, the pasture will become overgrazed and cease to support any cattle at all. So as human population increases, the number of cattle per family must fall, and a time must come when the family has to do something else to survive.

That something, for most people, was agriculture. Wherever Aryans went, we also find a system of cereal-based agriculture which incorporates cattle. It grows cereals as the main human food, and uses crop residues or fodder crops to maintain animals which help in farm work. This partnership of animals and men stretched from Europe in the west, through the Mediterranean and the crescent to India, and further down to South-East Asia. It spread to America when the Europeans colonized it. It had a distinct geographical boundary—the rice cultivators of China, the root cultivators of the Pacific, or the corn cultivators of the Americas were farmers, but they owned few or no cattle, they did not like milk, and they cultivated with human labour. North America swarmed with native buffaloes when Europeans first arrived there, but they were never domesticated.

Although the Aryans adapted their animal husbandry to the cattle they loved, they still faced competition between humans and cattle. Generally speaking, the less land there was to be farmed, the more cattle were kept. Around the Alps, there were foothills which could not be cultivated; they supported some of the finest cattle breeds. In the dry regions of north-west India, there was much land that was too dry to farm; it supported cattle, sheep and goats. Further south and east, as rainfall increased, more land was fit for cereal cultivation, and less land was available for cattle to roam. Hence people there found substitutes for ghee in vegetable oils. There may have been a time when India was a land of milk and honey; but by the early years of this century, it was a pretty poor country. Few could afford ghee, and many had turned to cheaper substitutes.

If a substitute is cheap enough and close enough, many people will abandon the real thing. In Europe, they had worked out a product that looked exactly like butter, tasted passably like it, but was made out of vegetable oils; it was called margarine. And if a butter-substitute could be made, a ghee-substitute could not be far behind. It was in fact made in the 1930s and introduced by Levers in India. It was christened vanaspati ghee or vanaspati for short; but most people knew it by the Levers' brand name of Dalda. It spread like wildfire; by the time of World War II, the government considered it essential enough to control its price. With controls, its price became simply the price of vegetable oils that went into it plus a processing margin. So it was much cheaper than ghee. By the 1950s, most restaurants and commercial establishments were using Dalda, and so were an increasing number of households. A family had to be rich to be using ghee.

Ghee fights back

In the past four decades, however, ghee has become cheaper in relation to all its competitors. Why is this?

The primary reason is to be found in the green and the white revolutions. The green revolution consists essentially of three things—high-yielding seeds, irrigation water, and nitrogenous fertilizer—coming together to raise the rate of growth of cereal production, principally that of wheat and rice. As cereal production rose, so did the production of stalks; straw production went up, thus increasing fodder supply.

But equally important, the increased output has raised farmers' incomes, and enabled them to buy tractors. Thirty years ago wise people laughed if anyone said that Indian agriculture would be tractorized; today, India is the world's biggest tractor producer. And every tractor replaces a pair of bullocks; or rather, it replaces fifty or 100 pairs. The bullocks that went out of use are no longer being fed, and more fodder has become available for milch cows and buffaloes. There has been much talk of the white revolution—of V. Kurien, the National Dairy Development Board, and the cooperatives having turned India into the world's second biggest milk producer. Actually, that achievement is due more to India's newly acquired tractors than to the genius or sweat of dairymen.

But there may be another factor as well. Agricultural products grow on land, and compete for land. Land is scarce and has to be paid for. Suppose the yield of a crop goes up. Then, in effect, each ton of it is using less land, and the land cost attributable to it will go down. If these land costs are reflected in prices, then the prices of those crops whose yields go up more will decline relatively to the prices of crops whose yields go up less. Since cattle eat straw, and the green revolution has been the most pronounced in wheat and rice, the land cost of milk has fallen relatively to that of other crops; that is reflected in its price. Mustard, on the other hand, competes for land with wheat; because it has not undergone a comparable green revolution, its land cost has gone up, and so has its relative price. Groundnuts, on the other hand, are produced on arid land in the peninsula which cannot be used for wheat and rice, so the price of groundnut oil has gone up less.

The fact is that apart from mustard and soyabean, all Indian vegetable oils are obtained from dry crops, which have suffered in the green revolution. If the land on which they were grown becomes irrigated, farmers turn to more lucrative crops such as cereals or sugar cane; as more land gets irrigated, the supply of dry land shrinks, and the land costs of dry crops go up. That is why vegetable oils have been getting so expensive.

And yet, Indians love fats. Those who cannot afford

ghee buy vanaspati; those who cannot buy vanaspati buy vegetable oils. So as they have got better off, they have been buying more vegetable oils. Domestic production has not kept up with demand; that is why domestic prices rose. As domestic prices rose, a gap opened between them and prices abroad. The government and its agencies made enormous profits from this in the 1980s; they imported oils cheap and sold them to their own population at the much higher domestic prices. Some of the oils were sold at lower prices through fair price shops; but that only created a chance for others to buy cheaply from the shop-owners and sell it dear. So a lot of money was made. But in the 1990s, ideas of reform began floating around, it become unfashionable to allow government agencies to make profits out of import restrictions, and the imports of vegetable oils were freed. The effect of this relaxation can be seen in the tails of the price lines in figure 4 sloping downward at the end.

CEREALS

If sugar is a luxury sinking into becoming a necessity, cereals are the quintessential necessity—in the sense that as people get richer, they spend a decreasing proportion of their income on cereals. Which also means that the poorer they are, the more important cereals are to them. We have an elaborate network of fair price shops to reach cereals to the poor. But their prices are a constant headache to the government as well as the buyers. The central government spends more on foodgrain distribution than it receives. Every few years it decides that the losses are unbearable, and gives the prices a sharp hike. In the meanwhile, the system reaches only a small part of the population, and its coverage of the poor is accidental and idiosyncratic.

Onions are a recognizable product; if you have seen one onion, you will recognize all. Sugar too is not too difficult to identify. Sugar abroad looks whiter than Indian sugar, and comes as powder, candy or cubes; but they all taste the same. Vegetable oils come in different colours, but feel the same—oily. Cereals come in more shapes and sizes. If you come across an unfamiliar grain—such as ragi or spelt—you may not recognize it; you may mistake it for birdseed. Maybe there are children in western countries who have never seen a foodgrain. But once told that something is a foodgrain, you would have no difficulty in recognizing it as such. Sorghum or millet is a worthy product in itself, but it is worth looking at all cereals together in view of the official attention they get, and the mythology that underlies that concern.

The hold of cereals on the food habits of people across the world is remarkable. Cereals are the commonest food, although they are not the dominant food of people everywhere. People in western countries eat a lot of meat; and there are ranching countries like Argentina where a beefsteak for breakfast, lunch and dinner might not be considered unusual. Cereals have been the mainstay of Asian countries; and most of them to our east have been rice-eaters. There too food habits have been changing. The Japanese still eat a lot of rice and fish; but as they have got richer in the past fifty years they have begun to import meat—mainly beef from Australia and America. The Chinese, who too are going through the same transition, are eating a lot more pork—and importing soyabean oilcake from India to feed the pigs. But India is the most devoted to cereals amongst all countries; it is also the only country in the world with a substantial population of vegetarians, for whom cereals are indispensable.

Mankind takes a wrong turn

Cereals were not always so important; in fact, there was a time only a few millennia ago when humans left them for the birds, for agriculture was then yet to be invented. Humans probably ate whatever was close at hand and where it was not, they hunted for food. There are archaeologists who rummage around in the rubbish heaps of extinct communities and work out what they ate; wild animals are invariably found to have been a very important part of the food. This impression may be due to the fact that animals leave a trace in the form of bones whereas snails or roots may not. But wild animals clearly played a large part in the lives of ancient people; the pictures they drew frequently show them pursuing deer and mammoths with spears, bows, arrows and other weapons. Meat and fish were fancied food. There are still small, isolated communities, for instance in the Amazon or the Andamans, who live by collecting; and they depend a good deal on hunting. And even today people eat more of both when they get richer. So what happened in between that gave cereals a place of such importance in human diets?

The trouble with a livelihood based on hunting is that it required enormous amounts of land per head. Look at the tiger; even in the most favourable locations each tiger would need 25 square kilometres if it is to have enough animals to eat; if the area available shrinks, it will eat up animals faster than they reproduce themselves and starve. As human population grew, people had to do something besides hunting to feed themselves. They had to confine animals and feed them; and they had to grow things to feed the animals as well as themselves.

Even then, if I had been involved in the collective decisions taken at the crossroads in dietetic history, I would have urged mankind to adopt nuts as their traditional food. Nuts are simply big seeds; they are full of the same carbohydrates and oils. Weight-conscious socialites may avoid them as too fatty; but they do not know that even rice yields oil, which is nowadays made into vanaspati and soap. Nuts, however, can be eaten without cooking, which is a terrible waste of time and energy; and they are so much tastier. I cannot help thinking that if humans had adopted a diet of walnut and cashew, pistachio and macadamia, almond and chestnut, they would have been a more cheerful race.

Maybe there was an age when humans were nut-eaters; but the inexorable growth of population that finished off the wild animals also made a substitute for nuts necessary. For trees have low yields; they need much land, and their growth cycle is slow. So after experimentation, humans came to grains as the best compromise. Their yields were high, and they required less land. Many of them yielded straw which could be fed to animals. Once dried, they were eminently transportable, and could feed cities; the most prominent feature of Mohenjo Daro was the granary. And they could be stored. In countries that had dry and wet or hot and cold seasons, food could be produced only during part of the year, and storability was important. Grains did not conquer the world. In equatorial areas where it rained all round the year, grain would not dry; these regions still eat quantities of roots such as taro, cassava and yam. The misty mountains of Colombia are the home of the potato, and produce four hundred varieties of them. But the river valleys of tropical and subtropical areas were taken over by cereals. And where once humans had painted pictures of hunting, they started organizing harvest festivals, praying to the sun and rain, and throwing rice in weddings. The basis of such rituals and the emotions that come to be associated with them is food anxiety. Humans work out a technology that feeds them, specialize in it, and worry that if it fails to deliver enough food, they will starve. The worry was no doubt based on real experience. In industrial countries where the possibility of food shortage has disappeared, the rituals too have atrophied; no emotion is invested in the activity of feeding oneself.

But in India, food shortages are within living memory. The Bengal famine of 1943 killed millions. Since then there has been no acknowledged famine. But I have myself been to villages in Bihar in 1966 where no men were left. Free kitchens were only for women and children, so men had either died or gone looking for work.

This experience of starvation makes food security such a live issue in India. In countries without such experience, no one, let alone the government, ever gives it a thought. In India, however, the government buys and sells millions of tons of cereals and distributes them through thousands of fair price shops in the name of food security and equitable distribution of food.

How did the government get into this?

Anyway, food security was not the motivation for the government entry into distribution. During World War II, the government began to purchase materials and engage people for the war. This government spending put rising incomes in people's hands, and their spending increased demand still further. This spiral of spending mainly affected towns, which began to draw goods from the countryside. There was a danger that so much of cereals would be sucked into the cities that villages would go short of food. So the government put a ban on the movement of cereals into cities, and instead began to buy wheat and rice from the countryside and selling them in towns. The intention was to restrain the townspeople's food consumption so that their poorer country cousins did not go without food.

That was the intention, but it was never quite realized. Despite food rationing, Bengal had a famine in 1943; and supplying enough grains to the towns remained a worrying problem throughout the war. Wartime was bad enough; but independence proved worse. A good deal of the wheat sold in rations was bought in west Punjab which went to Pakistan. The loss of that wheat supply put the rationing system in jeopardy. Rafi Ahmed Kidwai, who was then food minister, tried out an experiment: he abandoned rationing. But there were such shortages that he had to bring it back within months.

So rationing continued. Imperceptibly its function changed. Its original object was to prevent urban people from buying more food than they could live on, irrespective of what they were prepared to buy. But as they were prevented from buying as much as they could, villagers had also to be prevented from selling to them: private carriage of cereals into cities and from surplus to deficit provinces had to be prevented. Once this was done farmers had no choice but to sell their produce to the government, and the government could buy it up at a price below what would have ruled without rationing. Given the high demand in cities, the government could have made a tidy profit on its grain trade. But it did not; under the notion that it would thereby reduce inflation, the government sold the grains more or less at cost. Thus slowly, the objective changed from reducing the demand to reducing the price—and if you reduce the price below the market-clearing price, you actually increase the demand. A rationing system divorces prices from the market; it thus gives scope for the exercise of philanthropy at the expense of farmers, and for cross-subsidizing townspeople at the farmers' expense. As this happens, some farmers will find it unprofitable to grow cereals, while others will find greater profit in other crops. Thus the cross-subsidy reduces supply, and perpetuates the shortage even when the inflationary conditions that initially caused the shortage have passed. Rationing creates conditions which make its continuance necessary.

There was a short period in the early 1950s when food supply and demand were well matched and rationing could be relaxed. But in 1956 the government began an ambitious programme of industrialization which had similar effects to the war: it increased urban employment and incomes and built up demand for cereals. Rationing had to be brought back in full strength, and was used to underprice cereals, tax farmers and subsidize townspeople. A shortage of cereals developed.

During and after the War, the United States had been feeding first its allies and later its devastated ex-enemies in Europe. In the 1950s these European countries recovered and began to produce enough food for themselves. So the USA began to give wheat free to India; this wheat came to sustain the rationing system. American wheat looked and tasted different from Indian wheat; urban consumers sniffed, but ate it. There were people in the South who had never eaten wheat and did not know how to cook it; they tried to boil it like rice. Incidentally, boiled wheat is perfectly edible, and makes an excellent addition to a salad. But somehow it is unfashionable to eat it that way.

This patronal relationship between the US and India came under strain in the mid-1960s. India had refused to join the US in the ring it had thrown to contain the Soviet Union; and as Soviet–American relations worsened, the US began to resent this. The US wheat surplus also began to decline. The US began to give India signals that the flow of wheat could not continue—that India might have to pay for it, and that India should be growing more grains and less of something else, such as cotton. The Indian government regarded these signals as unfair pressure, and relations went from bad to worse.

Then came the poor harvest of 1965. The US shipped a record quantity of 11 million tons of wheat to India that year—India's foodgrain output was then just over 100 million tons a year—but made it clear that India had to make radical policy changes and reduce its dependence for food.

It just happened that the Bhakra-Nangal irrigation system, whose construction began in the mid-1950s, neared completion just then, and the new high-yielding variety of Mexican wheat developed by Borlaug in California reached India. In a masterstroke, C. Subramaniam, who was then minister of agriculture, concentrated the improved seeds and fertilizer on the irrigated areas of Punjab and started off a boom in wheat production which replaced American imports. The rest is history. India has never been a big importer of food since the 1960s. Food security became a part of national religion.

Crumbling fences

The rationing system had started as a means of preventing the townspeople from buying up too much grain and leaving villagers starving. In the years after the War, it underwent a subtle transformation: the system began to subsidize townspeople at the expense of farmers. Since farmers were paid less than they would get in the open market, they had to be forced to sell to the government. The government prevented them from selling off their surplus by prohibiting unauthorized movement of grain across districts and states.

The ingress of American wheat in the 1950s reduced the need for force; less needed to be bought from farmers. But otherwise the system continued as before. Instead of domestic surplus, imports were plugged in. Townspeople were subsidized by the American government as well. The subsidy perpetuated the shortage, and justified movement restrictions.

The green revolution changed all that; for the India-grown Mexican wheat soon turned from a trickle into an avalanche. In 1965 India produced 10 million tons of wheat. This rose to 20 million tons in 1969, 32 million tons in 1977, and 46 million tons in 1983; today India produces 70 million tons. The advance of wheat was spectacular, but the rise in rice production was not to be sniffed at; it rose from 30 million tons in 1966 to 40 million tons in 1969, 53 million tons in 1977, and 60 million tons in 1983. The need to stop townspeople from buying too much disappeared; instead, the problem was finding a means to create demand for such a vast quantity of grains. Exports were prohibited, so the market had to be found within the country. As a result, movement restrictions began to crumble. First, state governments stopped restricting movement across districts. Then, the central government allowed movement across states once its own procurement was over. In the 1990s, even the restrictions during the procurement season were abandoned. Next, the central government began to subsidize the ration sale of cereals from its own budget. Finally, some states like Tamil Nadu began to buy rice within their borders and sell it with a subsidy to their own consumers.

The rationing system began as a segmentation of markets: the urban market was cordoned off from the rural market, and urban consumers' demand was controlled to keep rural prices down. Today the cordon is gone. Only the West Bengal government tries to enforce it; and even it does not prevent small-scale carriage of grains. The result is that thousands of villagers crowd into trains to Calcutta after the harvest with bags of rice to sell. The two markets for grain—the public distribution system and the open market—are no longer segregated. One shop may be a fair price shop selling rice at Rs 6 a kilogram; next door may be a grocer selling the same rice at Rs 12. They may even belong to the same man.

That would be very convenient, for all he has to do is to get rice from the government at a price below Rs 6 and sell it at Rs 12. He would love such a business. What prevents him from doing it? He cannot do it because he is supposed to sell only to ration cardholders. Every consumer can get only one ration card.

A rationing inspector is supposed to visit every consumer before issuing him with a ration card and make sure the consumer exists and does not already have a ration card. The consumer could resell ration grains and make a profit; but as long as he needs them for his own consumption, he would not.

Thus the removal of the barriers between the ration areas and free market areas increases the responsibility of the administrators. They must ensure that cereals, once they are bought by the government and enter the public distribution system, do not leak into the open market until they are delivered to the cardholder. The points at which they might leak out are many. They might be stolen out of the godowns, many of which are just open areas where gunny bags of grain are stacked and guarded by a watchman or two. They may be pilfered from the trains and trucks that take them from the storage areas to the states where they are consumed. They may be sold off by the officials of the state food departments before they reach the fair price shops. And finally, the fair price shop-owner may have bogus cardholders on his list, and may sell off the grain he gets in their name.

Controls to prevent such diversion do not exist. So the public distribution system is something between a machinery that sells subsidized food to the poor and a business in which those involved make profits at the expense of the state and the taxpayer. It is neither fully one nor the other. The rationing system works better in some states than in others, in some cities than in others. But no one knows how well it works, and no one tries to find out—least of all the government. Typically, a consumer gets a ration card or a trader gets a licence to run a fair price shop on the recommendation of a legislator—a member of Parliament or Assembly. If they are not conscientious, they can easily introduce bogus consumers.

Narasimha Rao as Prime Minister announced that the rationing system would be extended to 1700 remote and backward blocks; under his rule, the offtake from the public distribution system doubled in five years. It may be that many new poor people are getting subsidized rations; but it is also possible that politicians have increased the share of the profits of diverting grain from the system into the open market.

The government never investigates the real state of affairs, so we do not know the level of corruption in the public distribution system. But there is one National Sample Survey which enables us to work out the level of subsidy that reaches the ration cardholders. In no state does it exceed Rs 12 per cardholder per month; in many states it is only Rs 3-4. The average income of cardholders at the time of the survey was about Rs 400 per month per head including every man, woman and child; there would be few families earning less than Rs 1500 a month. So even for the poor, the subsidy conveyed was small. There was no relationship between the incidence of poverty and the number of cardholders; the poorest states were the least covered. Thus the government machinery buys vast quantities of grains, stores them, carries them across the country and sells them to give benefits to cardholders which are modest even for the poorest of them.

There are other side-effects. Some of the most intensive users of the public distribution system are the north-eastern states. They border Bangladesh and Burma, and it is possible that the grains are smuggled out from there. There is also the inexorable decline in the output of grains other than wheat and rice. Jowar, bajra and ragi were important cereals eaten mainly by the poor; their share in foodgrain output has come down. Their decline is supposed to have been bad for the poor. This is uncertain. We Indians are consuming roughly 20 per cent more grain now than in the 1950s, and wheat and rice have become cheaper relatively to coarse grain. Hence it is likely that the poor have replaced coarse grains with wheat and rice. But the government provides an assured market for wheat and rice. It is possible that the ease of marketing has favoured the growth of these fine grains.

In the search for food security, we have found insecurity. Figure 5 shows the annual rise in the weighted wholesale price of wheat and rice, and the price at which the government buys them from farmers; it also shows how much government operations—procurement, distribution to ration shops, imports and exports—added to or reduced the population's foodgrain consumption per head per day. When the government injects grains into the market, the rate of inflation of wholesale prices comes down; when it withdraws grains, inflation shoots up.

And whenever the government releases grains, its stocks go down, it gets worried about the level of stocks, raises procurement prices, and begins to withdraw grains from the market. Briefly, the way government worries about excessive or inadequate stocks leads it to accelerate or decelerate the rise in the prices it pays farmers; the price it pays farmers draws grains into its own godowns and reduces market stocks, and the fall in market stocks raises market prices.

Thus, government intervention in the markets for cereals actually reduces the stability of prices. To ensure supplies at home, the government has banned foodgrain exports. Every few years there is an unmanageable surplus, export permits are issued, and markets are found at throwaway prices. The ban on exports keeps domestic foodgrain prices below those that rule abroad; when imports have to be made, they are bought at prices much above those given to our own farmers. They resent this, and press for ever higher prices. Under their pressure, procurement prices are raised every year; thus the government creates continuous inflation.

The need for rationing ended in the 1970s when the green revolution ended the foodgrain shortage; since then, public distribution has been unnecessary. It helps the poor very little; the subsidies it conveys are tiny. And food security can be bought by other means at a much lower cost. Food security requires that the food stocks in the country are sufficient to meet the highest conceivable year-to-year fluctuations in output. It is ensured if sufficient stocks are financed by means of cheap credit. It does not matter who holds the stock; it is better that the stocks should be held by traders who would buy them at the best price, at home or abroad, store them properly, and turn them over before they deteriorate.

Fig 5. Government operations in cereals

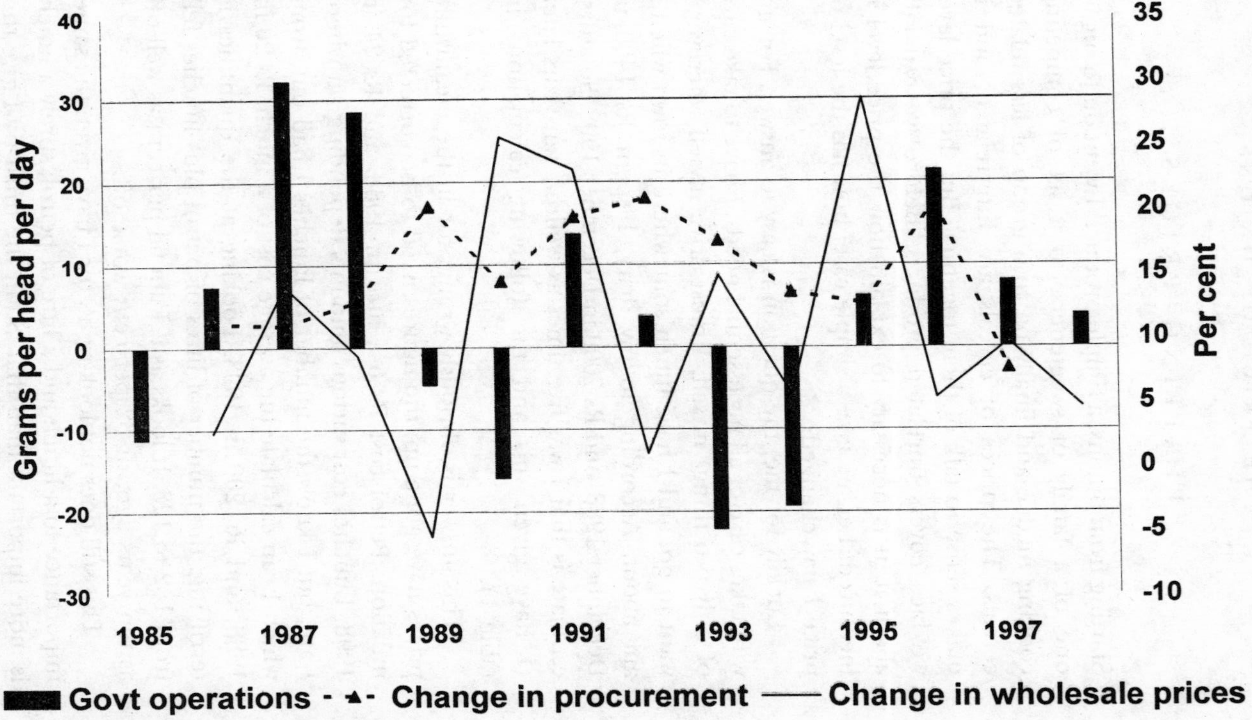

PLAITING PRICES

Starting from onions, a simple product, I went on to sugar, one of a family of sweeteners, to a set of competing cooking media, and finally on to a group of less related cereals. The prices of cereals are interrelated, and it makes sense to talk of them together. But the price level we face covers unrelated products. Before we can talk about it, it is necessary to explain how the price level is measured. Let me take a simple case: how has the level of price I pay changed?

Luckily for me, the question is easy to answer. For my wife takes care of all my essential needs. I have to take care of only two things myself; I must drive myself wherever I want to go, and I have lunch somewhere in town when I am about. According to my diary, I spent Rs 1400 in December 1988, and Rs 7000 in December 1998. So a first estimate is that I was five times as well off ten years later (I have given this and the following calculations in table 1).

This answer is obviously wrong, for in the meanwhile prices have gone up; the figures need to be corrected for inflation. Petrol cost Rs 6 a litre in 1988, and Rs 24 in 1998. Lunches cost various amounts depending on where I ate; but I know the number of lunches I had out, from which I can calculate the average cost of a lunch: Rs 20 in 1988, and Rs 200 in 1998. Looking at the quantities is terrifying: the number of litres of petrol plus lunches fell from 182 to 123. It looks as if I am 68 per cent as well off as ten years ago, or 32 per cent worse off.

This still does not look right, for I have given the same importance to a lunch and a litre of petrol; surely a lunch is more important than that. So in the third try I give the same importance to eating and to travel. That gives a somewhat more satisfying result: I am only 16 per cent worse off than ten years ago.

But I can do better than that. Lunches and travel are not equally important to me. Their importance is roughly reflected in what I spend on them. So in the fourth try I give them weights in proportion to my expenditure on them in 1988. Uh, huh! That does not look so good: now I am 24 per cent worse off than ten years ago.

Suddenly I am struck by the mistake I am making. Ten years ago I was driving a 1962 Fiat. A dear old car it was; but it gave me only 10 kilometres a litre. Now I whiz around in a Maruti 800, which gives me 16 kilometres a litre. What I am enjoying is not litres of petrol my car burns up but kilometres of driving; and I am driving exactly the same distance as ten years ago. So I equalize the distance driven in 1988 and 1998, and my standard of living jumps up forthwith: I am now 14 per cent better off than ten years ago.

At last I can conclude I am better off. But I still do not feel happy; I feel a lot more better off than 14 per cent. Then it strikes me: the pocket money my wife gave me ten years ago was so meagre that I mostly ate chhole-kulche or rice-rajma standing at a streetside stall. When I felt rich I went to a mat-and-thatch hovel serving sturdy Punjabi peasant food, tried to grab a table in front of the solitary pedestal fan, and washed down the lunch with a lassi. Whereas nowadays I think nothing of going to a Japanese restaurant, air conditioned and licensed. This change in my quality of life must somehow be reflected in the calculation.

I introduce it in the sixth try by distinguishing between lunches that serve the duty of feeding oneself and lunches that are a delight. In 1988, twenty out of the twenty-two lunches were in dhabas; in 1998, I had fifteen of the twenty-three lunches in posh restaurants. Once I give

TABLE 1

How much better off am I?

	weight	1988 Price (Rs)	1988 Consumed	1988 Spent (Rs)	1998 Price (Rs)	1998 Consumed	1998 Spent* (Rs)	Times better off
First try								
Total Expenses				1400			7000	7000/1400=5.00
Second try								
Petrol		6	160 ltrs	6x160=960	24	100 ltrs	24x100=2400	
Lunches		[20]	22	20x22=440	[200]	23	200x23=4600	
			182	960+440=1400		123	2400+4600=7000	123/182=0.68
Third try								
Petrol			1000			1000x100/160=625		
Lunches			1000			1000x23/22=1045		
			2000			625+1045=1670		1670/2000=0.84
Fourth try								
Petrol	960/1400=0.686		1000	0.686x1000=686		625	0.686x625=429	
Lunches	440/1400=0.314		1000	0.314x1000=314		1045	0.314x1045=328	
				686+314=1000			429+328=759	759/100=0.76
Fifth try								
Kilometres driven	0.686		1000	686		1000	686	
Lunches	0.314		1000	314		1045	329	
				1000			1014	1014/1000=1.014
Sixth try								
Kilometres driven		6/10=0.6	1600	960	24/16=1.5	1600	2400	
Visits to dhabas		300/20=15	20	300	400/8=50	8	400	

	weight	1991 Price (Rs)	1991 Consumed	1991 Spent (Rs)	1998 Price (Rs)	1998 Consumed	1998 Spent (Rs)	Times better off
Pleasurable lunches		140/2=70 1400 7000	2	140	4200/15 280	15	4200	
Laspeyres Index								
Kilometers driven	960/1400=0.686		1000	686		1000	686	
Visits to dhabas	300/1400 = 0.214		1000	214		400	86	
Pleasurable lunches	140/1400=0.100		1000	100		7500	750	
				1000			1521	1.52
OR								
Kilometers driven		0.6	1600	960	0.6	1600	960	
Visits to dhabas		15	20	300	15	8	120	
Pleasurable lunches		70	2	140	70	15	1050	
				1400			2130	1.52
Paasche Index								
Kilometers driven	2400/7000=0.343		1000	343		1000	0.343x1000=343	
Visits to dhabas	400/7000=0.057		2500	143		1000	0.057x1000=57	
Pleasurable lunches	4200/700=0.600		133	80		1000	0.600x1000=600	
				566			1000	1.77
OR								
Kilometers driven		1.5	1600	2400	1.5	1600	2400	
Visits to dhabas		50	20	1000	50	8	400	
Pleasurable lunches		280	2	560	280	15	4200	
				3960			7000	1.77

separate weights to cheap and luxurious lunches, the jump in my standard of living rises to a respectable 52 per cent.

At this point I realize that the comparison I have been making is backward looking; I have been assuming that my consumption basket in 1988 was the standard and the 1998 basket had to be weighed against it. I could equally regard my 1998 basket as the standard and ask myself how much bigger it was than the one ten years ago. So in the seventh try, I replace the weights based on expenditure in 1988 by ones based on expenditure in 1998. The results improve; according to this backward-looking calculation, I am 1.77 times as well off in 1998 as in 1988.

There is little to choose between the forward- and backward-looking estimates—1.52 and 1.77. At this point I find no pointer that can take me forward. So I look up a textbook. It says that the forward-looking index was invented by a German called Etienne Laspeyres in 1864 and is called the Laspeyres index after him, and the backward-looking index is called the Paasche index after Hermann Paasche, another German statistician who invented it in 1874. Neither is better than the other. If one has to settle on a single number, one might, for lack of a better alternative, choose Fisher's ideal index, named after Irving Fisher who invented it in the 1920s. This is the geometric mean of the Laspeyres and the Paasche indexes—in my case, 1.64. After 1924 there have been many sophisticated advances in index-making. But almost all the indexes calculated, published and used in the world are Laspeyres indexes; so we can stop our education in 1864.

Duet of Paasche and Laspeyres

Paasche indexes are no worse than their Laspeyres cousins, and might in fact be preferable sometimes. Suppose, for example, that instead of continuing to eat cheap lunches sometimes, I had switched entirely to posh lunches. Then the number of cheap lunches I ate would have fallen to zero in 1998, and the Laspeyres index would have counted only the change in kilometres driven, and not risen at all. In other words, it would have shown that my standard of living was the same in 1988 and 1998. The Paasche index would have shown an enormous improvement in my standard of living: it would have shown me to be 3.69 times as well off in 1998 as in 1988. Neither would have been terribly accurate, but I would think that the second figure came closer to reality.

The problem of disappearing or emerging commodities is endemic in calculation of standards of living, gross domestic product, industrial production etc. For instance, when I learnt indexes forty years ago, there were no computers. My prize possession was a German slide rule. My father's greatest gift to me was that he had taught me multiplication tables up to 40, so that I could tell without a moment's thought that 37 by 9 was 333. When I went abroad to study, I encountered the first electric calculators—machines as big as kittens, which clattered like overage trucks, but which could cumulate sums of products. With them I could calculate an index within minutes, and a regression within a day—but to make sure I had not made a mistake, I had to calculate the regression three times—and if I did not get the same answer, a fourth time. Today my laptop does a regression in seven seconds.

Worse was to come when I had wasted a couple of years doing regressions and written up a weighty thesis. Then it had to be typed, and the typist had to make multiple carbon copies for examiners. They would not have been pleased had there been typing errors. So one had to find a faultless typist. An accurate typist was worth her weight in gold and cost as much; that is why the wives of so many professors started as their typists. For laptop of today, read typist of yesteryears.

Not everyone may regard computers a great advance in human civilization. But half a century ago there were no zips; all garments had to be buttoned. There was no television; instead, there were radio addicts. There were no stereo sets; the only way of listening to good music was to go to a concert. There was no plastic; since leather was expensive, most people in India went about barefoot. Air conditioning was prohibitively expensive; that is why the Bombay High Court chambers open out to verandas, which kept the sun away and wafted cool air in. The only synthetic fibres were rayon and nylon; they were so expensive that women prized them more than Conjeevaram silk. Only big bureaucrats and businessmen had cars. Of the rest, the young flew about on bicycles, while the old took a tonga if they could afford it, and walked if they could not. Every city had a clock tower because few could afford a watch. Clock towers were called bell towers (ghanta ghar) because chimes were a must—if the clocks had been silent, everyone would have had to walk to the town centre every few hours to find out if it was tea-time.

So if someone made a 1950-based Laspeyres index of the Indian standard of living today, the base would exclude many products that matter a lot to us today, and would grossly underestimate the rise in the standard of living. A Paasche index would reflect our living conditions better.

Still, official bodies universally prefer Laspeyres indexes because Paasche indexes are too troublesome. A Paasche index would require one to estimate weights based on current patterns of consumption—let us say, every year. Weighting is an elaborate ritual in the government. It appoints an expert committee consisting of great professors and little bureaucrats from all corners of India, they meet once a quarter to deliberate and dine, and take years to decide a new weighting pattern. By the time they finish, it is time to appoint another committee to work out the next pattern. The best that such ways of working can achieve is to update the weights of a Laspeyres index once every few years. The base of the index of industrial production was recently changed from 1980-81 to 1990-91. The committee to do so was appointed in 1991, reported in 1996, and the weights were changed in 1997. Soon it will be a new millennium, and time for a new committee.

But there is one exception—the Bombay Stock Exchange (BSE). It brings out an index of share prices called the Sensitive Index or Sensex. Sensex covers thirty shares; the shares are the ones most heavily traded on the stock exchanges, and their prices are weighted in proportion to their market capitalization—that is, the product of their prices and the total shares issued. BSE reweights the Sensex every day; the weight of shares whose market capitalization has gone down is reduced, and shares whose market capitalization has gone up increase their weight. Thus over the years, the Sensex has a bias towards shares whose prices—and hence market capitalization—have gone up. That is why the Sensex was 3000 in 1996 and 3000 in 1999, but the value of your share portfolio fell from Rs 3,00,000 to Rs 1,00,000. They would tell you you chose the wrong shares; maybe you did, but today's Sensex is not the one you met in your youth.

Laspeyres and Paasche indexes are close cousins. For instance, my expenses rose five-fold between 1988 and 1998. If I divided this by the Laspeyres index of my standard of living, I would get the Paasche index of the inflation I have suffered, and vice versa. If my standard of living went up 1.52 times according to the Laspeyres index, the prices I paid must have gone up by 3.29 times; if my standard of living went up 1.77 times, the prices must have gone up by 2.82 times.

That, at least, was what I had learnt in school. But when I calculated the actual inflation, I got higher figures of inflation—the Paasche index came out as 3.95, and the Laspeyres index as 3.58 (table 1). I was thrilled; I thought I had disproved a fundamental statistical theorem. But then I had another look at the figures; the truth was more mundane. What I was buying was petrol, but what I was enjoying was kilometres. If I calculated the price indexes in terms of kilometres driven, they turned out to be properly related to the quantity indexes. But different people would get different mileage from a litre of petrol; the government cannot make up a separate index for each. If I ignored the fact that I was getting more mileage from a litre, then inflation turned out to be higher.

This point may seem to be rather arcane, but the Americans have just discovered how important it is. Their price indexes have ignored the fact that the quality of goods and services has been improving and that people have been getting more 'mileage' out of them. They reckon that this ignored rise in standard of living is of the order of 1 per cent a year. For decades, the American standard of living has risen at about 2 per cent a year. At that rate, their standard of living would have risen 2.7 times in half a century; at 3 per cent, it would have risen 4.4 times. Thus they have actually been getting better off much faster than they think. This must be true for all countries, including India, where goods and services serve better than before.

That is enough about the pitfalls of thinking about composite commodities; let us now see how fast this composite commodity called national output per head has been rising.

Growth and inflation

Figure 6 shows forty-eight years' record of inflation and rise in incomes per head from 1950-51 to 1998-99. During this period, the average income for Indians rose almost threefold; prices rose almost twenty-two-fold. No wonder that people are so much more concerned with prices than with incomes. Income may or may not rise; but in everybody's experience, prices rise all the time. And they rise so rapidly that your living standards can get rapidly eroded if income fails to rise.

This was not always so. There have been periods in India's history when prices rose very little. The nineteenth century was a period of very low inflation: prices fell as often as they rose, and no one regarded inflation as inevitable.

But things changed after World War II; most countries came to have some inflation all the time. One great change after the War was in the level of employment. During the War, all industrial countries were short of workers, and inducted large numbers of women into the work force. The high demand for workers continued after the War. To relieve the shortage, many prosperous countries imported workers: that is how Punjabis and West Indians went to Britain, Turks to Germany, and Latin Americans to the US. Labour scarcity increased workers' bargaining power, which they used to raise wages. A custom grew up of annual negotiations between trade unions and employers leading to wage increases. Since wages rose faster than productivity, production costs increased every year, and employers pushed up prices.

Fig 6. Rise in income per head and in prices

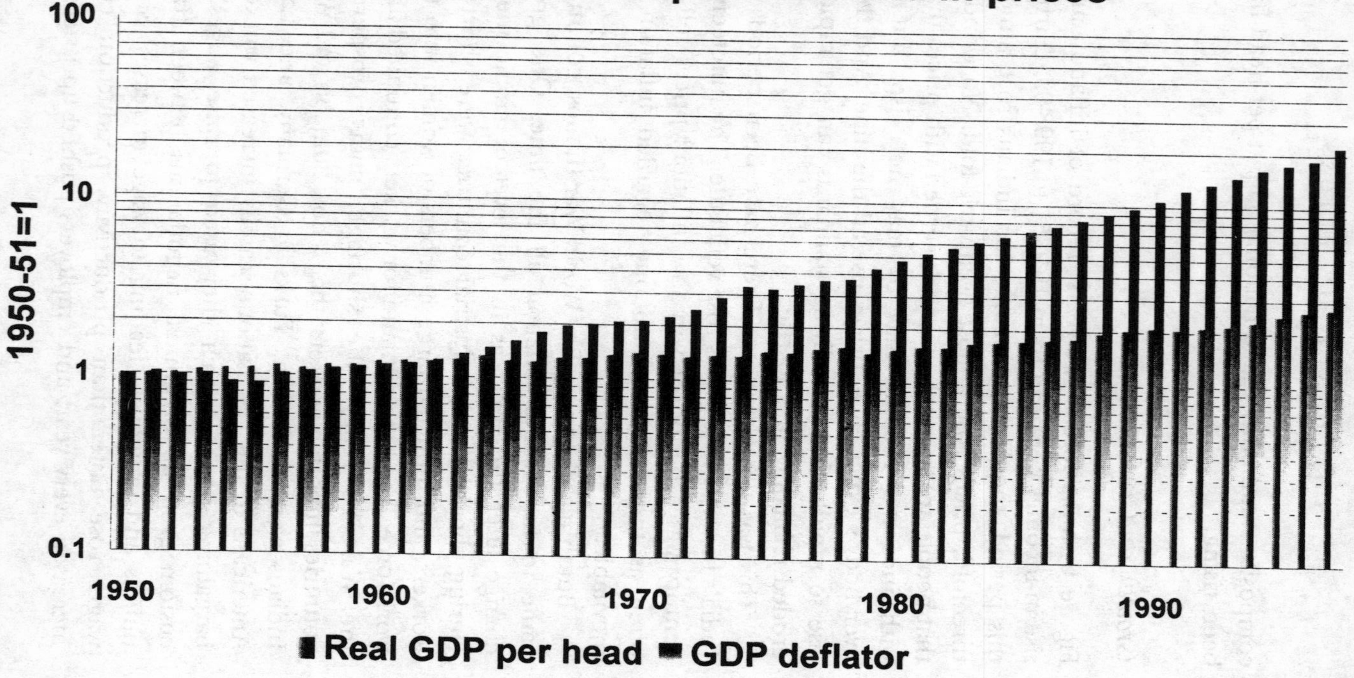

Apart from raising prices, these cost increases made exports uncompetitive and pulled in imports, and thus caused balance of payments crises in countries where productivity increase was slow. Some countries such as Britain and Sweden tried to restrain cost and price increases by getting employers and workers to restrain their demands. But that did not work too well.

Then came the oil crisis of 1973, when the Arab countries suddenly quadrupled prices of crude oil. The economies of industrial countries were shaken up. When they emerged out of the crisis, the problem of inflation feeding upon itself, with wage increases following upon as well as leading to price increases, died out in one country after another. In European countries, unemployment grew and weakened trade unions; in Japan, efficiency increases outstripped increases in money income; in the United States, the big unionized industries like steel and cars came under severe competition from imports, while employment grew in smaller firms. Today, there is very little inflation in industrial countries; in fact, many are more worried by slow growth than by price rise.

Industrial trade unions are neither so large nor so strong in India, and can hardly explain the chronic inflation. There have been years—1965-66, 1974-75, 1979-80, 1990-91—when income per head actually declined; those were also years of high inflation. But otherwise growth and inflation show little correlation. Inflationary forces live a life of their own independent of the forces of growth; but when growth falls very low for some reason—usually a balance of payments problem or a poor crop—inflation shoots up.

There are signs, however, that something changed around 1980. Growth has risen, and so has inflation. In figure 6, both GDP per head and inflation begin to rise faster from that year onwards, and their rise becomes more steady. The growth of income per head between 1951 and 1981 was just 1.5 per cent a year. That plus a 2 per cent growth rate of population gave 3.5 per cent growth of total income, which Raj Krishna christened the Hindu rate of growth. After 1980, however, the growth of per capita income has averaged 3.4 per cent, and it has been much more stable. Consequently, income per head rose 1.5 times in the first thirty years, and 1.8 times in the next eighteen years. Strangely, inflation has also risen from 5.5 per cent to 8.8 per cent, and it too has become more stable.

In the 1950s and 1960s when industrial countries suffered from chronic inflation, there were economists who thought inflation was good for growth. As inflation died out, so did they. Now this view is to be encountered in India. But extreme scepticism is the best treatment for this view. It is true that when supply suddenly falls, as in the Indian crises, prices shoot up. It is also true that when total demand falls short of supply, as in Japan today, prices cease to rise and may even fall. But in between these extremes, real events (that is, events relating to real goods and services independent of prices) and monetary events go their own separate ways.

If we knew how to control inflation, the ideal state would be if all cost reductions were passed on in price reductions. That way, the purchasing of the buyers' incomes would increase, they would be able to buy more goods and services even without a rise in their money incomes, and the benefit of cost reductions would spread throughout the economy. That is not how it always happens; workers whose productivity increases are bound to think that they must be rewarded for the cost reduction they have achieved. If there is keen competition in the product and labour markets, cost reductions are likely to be passed on to consumers. This is the case for promoting competition; it distributes the fruits of productivity rise more evenly and equitably across the population.

One would think that the millions of farmers could never combine and hold up prices and that reductions in their costs would pass on to their consumers; conversely, that industrialists would find it easy to conspire and keep up prices. The strange thing, however, is that agricultural prices have risen much faster than industrial prices since 1980. Imagine a composite industrial product constructed in proportion to the production of various industrial goods, and a similarly constructed agricultural product. The relative price of such an industrial product to that of the agricultural product today is only 77 per cent of what it was in 1980-81; that is, the producer of the composite agricultural product can buy 30 per cent more industrial products.

The change is so large and so persistent that it can happen only if industrial costs are rising less fast than agricultural costs—in other words, if industrial productivity is rising faster. But it is also possible that government intervention in foodgrain markets removes competition. The governments interpose monopoly buyers between the farmer and the consumer. These monopoly buyers influence market prices in such a way that competitive cost reduction amongst farmers would not be reflected in prices.

What would be the impact of higher agricultural prices than would rule in competitive markets? The purchasing power of buyers of agricultural goods—especially urban consumers and consumers of agro-based industrial goods, such as sugar, tobacco and cotton cloth—would be lower, and so would be their demand for goods and services. Farmers would get a higher price; but their incomes would not necessarily be raised. That would depend on how much higher prices reduce the demand for agricultural goods. If the demand were highly sensitive to price changes, higher prices would actually reduce farmers' incomes. Consumers in industrial countries spend so little on food that a rise in its price does not much affect demand for it. But in India, it is perfectly possible that lower prices for sugar, cloth, cigarettes, tea etc. would lead to higher incomes for farmers. If it did, price support for agriculture would reduce the incomes of both the producers and consumers of agricultural goods: it would reduce total income.

II

Nuts and Bolts of Bliss

At the end of the millennium, the average income of an Indian is about Rs 20,000 a year. The average income of an American is roughly $30,000 or Rs 12,00,000—about sixty times an Indian's income. Comparisons with other advanced countries are only a bit less startling. The question that arises in many Americans' minds is: how do Indians live on so little? They make up by imagination what they lack in knowledge: they have a simple picture of poor, starving Indians in their minds. Indians similarly make up the answer to the question: how do the Americans manage to consume over sixty times as much as Indians, when both have the same twenty-four hours a day and 365 days a year to do it? The most straightforward misconception to have is that the Americans waste a lot.

This comparison is a bit reminiscent of my naïve first attempts, described in Chapter 1, to measure how much better off I had become: because I was spending five times as much, I thought I was five times better off. That was, of course, wrong, for in the meanwhile, prices had risen; if I discounted my expenditure for the rise in prices, I got a rise in my standard of living that was much more modest.

The same fallacy applies to a comparison of the Indian and the American standards of living: the prices paid in the two countries differ. If the goods and services produced by the two countries are valued at the same prices, the difference is greatly narrowed. The United Nations does this comparison at common prices every once in a while. The latest I have is one for 1985 (United Nations and Commission of European Communities, World Comparisons of Real Gross Product and Purchasing Power, 1985, New York, 1994). It puts the US income per head at local prices at $16,484, and India at $350—a difference of 58:1; but when valued at the same prices, the US and Indian incomes per head were $16,484 and $794—a difference of 22:1.

These purchasing-power-parity (PPP) comparisons involving India started with a huge exercise organized by the World Bank in the 1970s. The original study is now almost twenty-five years old. But its antiquity does not matter; if it was done today, it would give similar results. In 1973, the average income of an Indian was Rs 1000; an American's income was $6192, or Rs 48,000. The difference was somewhat less than the present 60:1. More importantly, the Indians' average income in 1973 was $129; when, however, its purchasing power was valued at American prices, it rose to $394. Thus if prices were equalized, the difference of 48:1 shrank to 16:1.

That sounds better; but not a lot. Even a difference of 16:1 is large: it still needs a leap of imagination to conceive how the Americans lived sixteen times as well as we did.

Again, the example of the rise in my standard of living, in the last chapter, gives us some leads. For instance, just as I began to spend a smaller share of my expenditure on running around and more on eating out, the Americans might be spending more on things that cost more. Also, just as I graduated from eating in cheap joints to lunching in style, they may consume a better quality of the same things: they may cruise around in larger, better upholstered cars while I flit around in my mosquito, as the bus drivers call the Maruti; or they may snorkel in Mauritius while I sit on the beach in Mangalore.

Anyway, let me stop speculating and start looking at the figures in table 2. Incidentally, the table excludes items whose average Indian consumption is less than 1 per cent—more precisely, 0.5 per cent—of average American consumption, for instance, cars or washing machines.

TABLE 2

Quantities consumed and prices paid by an average Indian as a proportion of those consumed by an average American in 1973 (per cent)

	Qty	*Price*		*Qty*	*Price*
Food	14	58.1	Footwear	2	49.5
Rice	980	58.2	Rent	3	23.1
Flour	236	43.7	Repairs to houses	11	4.5
Beef	1	35.9	Fuel and power	3	49.5
Lamb	20	49.5	Furniture & appliances	1	67.1
Pork	1	26.1	Carpets	1	20.1
Fish	30	15.6	Refrigerators	1	182.8
Milk	25	36.9	Utensils	6	59.9
Eggs	3	68.9	Domestic services	34	3.1
Butter	10	51.7	Household services	42	14.3
Edible oils	26	98.3	Medical care	6	9.8
Tropical fruit	98	36.3	Hospitals	11	2.6
Fresh vegetables	43	75.0	Doctors	11	1.7
Tubers	18	43.5	Dentists	3	0.1
Tea	6	35.1	Nurses	3	60.6
Coffee	1	135.0	Vehicles	0	110.8
Sugar	16	94.5	Hired transport	25	48.8
Salt and spices	61	24.8	Rail transport	182	28.4
Beverages	1	120.3	Bus transport	239	25.9
Spirits	4	123.9	Communications	3	16.1
Beer	5	128.6	Recreation	1	39.4

	Qty	Price		Qty	Price
Nonalcoholic drinks	1	68.6	Education	11	9.5
Tobacco	6	77.3	Schoolteachers	29	4.3
Cigarettes	2	104.8	College teachers	9	9.9
Bidis, cigars etc	73	35.1	Educational books	15	31.1
Clothing	4	68.5	Stationery	1	31.2
Cloth	173	74.6	Personal care	2	55.9
Men's underwear	12	23.4	Barbers & beauticians	5	17.0
Women's underwear	1	73.4	Official compensation	22	6.2
Clothing repairs	4	16.4	Govt. commodities	3	30.5

Perhaps the most striking revelation of table 2 is that there are things of which Indians actually consume more than Americans. For instance, Indians eat almost ten times as much rice as Americans. It would not do to say that Indians are rice-eaters whereas Americans are wheat-eaters, because Indians also eat more than twice as much flour as Americans. What is happening is that Americans buy the same thing in a more finished form. Indians buy wheat, take it to the miller, take the flour home and bake it into rotis, Americans avoid all that rigmarole by simply buying bread. Thus Americans buy goods which embody more services—for instance, bread which embodies baking—whereas Indians buy less finished goods and use their own labour to finish them. In this case, the conventional calculation of national income includes only goods and services that are bought and sold, and thus underestimates that part of income which consists of doing something for one's own satisfaction.

Similarly, Indians buy almost twice as much cloth as Americans. In India we often go and buy cloth, and either wear it without any further ado—for instance, a sari, a dhoti or a shawl—or stitch it ourselves, or take it to our neighbourhood tailor to turn into baggy trousers or clinging cholis. Americans simply walk into a department store and buy clothes off the shelf. Here Americans are buying a more finished product. We buy it less finished and get it finished in another shop. Why? Because there are neighbourhood tailors in India, and none in America. Because labour is cheaper in India, many more people work in providing services. It is not so much that Indians spend a higher proportion of their incomes on services; the share of services in national income is lower in India. Rather, manual services are cheaper in India; hence Indians buy more services, and a wider range of services.

A third set of products of which Indians consume more than Americans is rail and bus services. This is straightforward substitution of a better or more convenient form—travelling in one's own car—for a less convenient one—hired transport—at a higher level of income.

Once we go beyond the exceptional items of which Indians consume more, however, things get more intriguing. Why for instance do we drink so much milk, give ourselves so much more education, pay our government servants so much? Let us take a look at the major heads of consumption to see what is happening.

FOOD

Man is supposed to be an animal that uses tools. That, at least, is how early anthropologists liked to describe mankind. Later it was discovered that animals too sometimes used tools. Monkeys poke a stick into an anthill, and lick up the ants that are stupid enough to run up the stick. Animals even have a bizarre sense of fun. Crows were recently photographed placing stones on the rails of the Japanese fast train, Shinkansen, to make it derail.

Now that the tool-based definition has been displaced,

I would like to describe mankind as the cooking animal. How humans started cooking is a subject lost in antiquity. But why they continue to cook is easier to answer. Cooking is a form of predigestion; it completes a part of the process of chemical disintegration that food undergoes in the stomach. In this way, cooking saves energy used in digestion; it makes more energy available for other activities, and quite possibly allows human beings to live on less food. It no doubt also makes the teeth last longer. Most of our ancient ancestors were dead by the time they were thirty, and many had lost their teeth by then. This is why virtually all known human tribes cook their food.

But cooking is not a purely utilitarian activity; it also modifies the taste of food. It enables the cook to extend the range of taste; it enhances the pleasure of consuming food. It turns a necessity into a luxury. In fact, cooked or processed food is one of the most widely available luxuries, and all humans spend considerable time, effort or income on it.

As societies get richer, their food undergoes three changes. First, the way they cook changes. Second, the range of foods they eat expands. Third, cooking or processing becomes a specialized, industrial activity.

Cooking in style

One of my most memorable sights is that of Masai women cooking. These denizens of the Kenyan highlands are tall and thin; women wear a stack of metal necklaces which makes them look taller. Driving around the scrub, I suddenly came across a group of Masai women. They had tied an ox by the legs, strung it up upside-down on a tree, and lit a bonfire under it. Little was required beyond brute female strength in this form of cooking.

Less spectacular, but equally shorn of sophistication,

was the Maori process of cooking I saw in Rotorua in New Zealand. Rotorua sits on a steaming reservoir. As one drives into the town, one encounters potholes in the roads through which steam rises. In the middle of the town is a steaming lake. There, in the rocks, are holes full of perpetually boiling water. The Maoris I saw tied a string to some meat and vegetables, and lowered them into the steaming holes; after a few minutes the fare was ready for eating.

Somewhat more elaborate is ceremonial Fijian cooking. Fijians make a hole in the ground, lay some charcoal at its bottom and light it. They then roll pieces of meat and fish as well as roots like taro and cassava in leaves, place them in the pit, and cover it up with earth. The fire, starved of air, smoulders. After half a day or so they open the pit, and eat the smoked victuals. There was a time they prepared enemies for eating in the same way. They ate everything else by hand, but for human beings they used special long wooden forks. Although baked legs have vanished forever, prototypes of the forks are sold as souvenirs to tourists. There was this Fijian friend of mine who was going to Britain on a boat from Sydney. On the way, his Australian fellow-passengers used to point at him and whisper: 'That is the great-grandson of the cannibal king of Fiji.' One evening at dinner, Ratu (Chief) Sitiveni Cakobau (pronounced Dhakombao) called the waiter, and said loudly, 'Waiter! This menu is boring; bring me the passenger list.'

Anyway, cooking for most people is not so effortless as for the Maoris of Rotorua. Unless they live near hot springs—or volcanos—they have to find kindling, set it alight, and tend the fire until the food is cooked just right—neither undercooked nor burnt. A Fijian feast would be ruined if it rained; and it rains a lot in Fiji. Primitive cooking requires too much fuel, too much skill and too much attention. So humans look for ways of reducing all the three inputs.

A matter of containment

The way in which fuel is economized is by concentrating the fire upon the food and reducing wasted heat; this is what all stoves and ovens do. But for efficient targeting, the food itself has to be confined; hence the use of utensils. Vessels are the most ubiquitous invention of mankind; much art and love went into their designs. Ancient civilizations are identified by the style of their pottery; for instance, the dominant Indian post-Harappan culture is known by its painted grey ware. The ancient Greeks made pale orange vessels, and painted scenes from their voyages, their battles, and their fairy tales on their amphorae (wine jars). The Chinese under the Ming dynasty mixed bone powder in the porcelain and made white tableware on which they painted exquisite pictures in blue.

These were vessels for storage and eating; but most earthen vessels were used for cooking. This is difficult to realize now; but for most of its history, most of mankind cooked in earthen pots. Copper, the commonest vessel of that time, was not strong enough to withstand repeated heating; iron was too expensive, and aluminium was unknown. Earthen cooking vessels were commonly used by the poor in India well into my own lifetime; it is only in the past fifty years that the poorest have changed over to aluminium vessels. The changeover could easily have saved them a third of the fuel they used earlier.

A vessel makes another improvement possible: it can hold water. Water surrounds food more evenly; and its temperature cannot exceed 100°C. Hence food cooked in water cannot burn; and heat penetrates it more deeply.

This is why boiling and steaming gained over roasting. It is only in recent times that the flow and temperature of dry heat has become controllable, and it is increasingly used for food processing—for instance, to make the ever-popular potato wafers and popcorn. This is also the process behind many ready-cooked foods or foods which require minimum cooking, such as ten-minute rice and noodles.

Vegetable oil and animal fat can also be used to cook food without burning it. They impart their own taste to the food; and since they contain 2¼ times as much energy per gram as carbohydrates, they make quite filling—and fattening—dishes. In old times when people did a lot of physical work, fried food was quite appropriate, and prized. It is only in our sedentary times that it has lost its charm.

Indian genius lies in its having combined boiling and frying. Boiling is cheap since water is much cheaper than cooking oil, but it gives an insipid product. Frying is expensive, and was probably not a process for everyday use in old times. Oil and water do not mix; you cannot boil and fry food at the same time. Our forefathers, however, added a medium—flour or a root like tapioca or potato—which could absorb oil and form a gravy. The gravy can also act as the vehicle for other flavouring agents such as spices. This is what the Indian curry is about. By now this style of cooking has spread across the world—it is common throughout South-East Asia, it has spread to the east coast of Africa, and China and Latin America have their own variants of it. But India is the Mecca of curry.

Advances in pyrotechnics

Confining heat, concentrating it on the food, using media to control cooking and impart flavours—these are all ancient inventions. What has changed in the industrial age is the fuel. Before the mid-nineteenth century, cooking fuel was solid—chiefly wood and straw. There are enormous variations in the quality of biofuels. The common element in all of them which burns and gives heat is carbon, but it is mixed with all sorts of other things. There are minerals, chiefly silicon, which when burnt turn into ash. There is water which turns into steam when heated; its conversion into steam absorbs considerable heat, leaving little for the food to be cooked. Moist wood also generates smoke when burnt; woods contain resins and other materials, which pass into and add to the smoke. That is why wood has to be dry to be useful. Straw has a high mineral content; it burns quickly and gives little heat. The best fuels are dense hardwoods; they give a lot of heat per gram. But they burn slowly; they are no good for processes like frying which require a lot of heat delivered quickly. There was an entire art of lighting a fire which has been lost with the modernization of cooking.

The choice of fuel is itself as complex a matter as cooking itself, especially since it is conditioned by availability. Intellectuals began to take interest in the question in the 1970s when the oil crisis made biofuels interesting as a substitute. The amounts of woody fuel being burnt for cooking were estimated; they were huge, and were quickly related to deforestation, which everyone is against. But amongst anti-deforestationists, three opinions emerged. One was the straightforward one which blamed ignorant country-dwellers for finishing off the earth's valuable stocks of wood. Another distinguished between good and bad villagers. There were virtuous villagers who harvested trees for fuel—who took only twigs, allowing trees to grow more. Then there were the bad villagers who kept goats; these voracious animals finished off all vegetation and turned the countryside into desert. The third school blamed city-dwellers for deforestation. They needed so much timber for doors, windows, fittings, scaffoldings, sleepers and so on, and contractors who supplied their needs descended on forests and cleaned them up like vultures.

Being large of heart, I believe all these schools are right—or have been right in some places at some times. The jungles of north India were cut down in the nineteenth century to fuel the first railways. The forests of eastern United States were cleared to grow grain. The forest of the Amazon is being cut down to make way for ranches. If the Masais continue to roast oxen strung on trees, they must need a lot of wood for fuel. Wood is useful, and land can be put to more valuable uses than leaving it forested.

As population grows denser, wooded area shrinks, both because agriculture feeds more people per hectare, and because the population outruns the supply of wood. And the population adjusts itself to the growing scarcity of wood. We could see this adaptation at work in India till recently. Amongst foodgrains, as we travelled from the green South and East towards the dry North and West, the pygmy crop of rice gave way to the tall bajra and jowar. These crops gave much more straw and hence fuel than rice or wheat. Indian wheat itself used to be taller—1.5 to 2 metres tall, as against rice which is less than a metre tall. The high-yielding varieties of Mexican wheat which are grown today are distinctly shorter. Besides, the North and the West grew woody crops such as dal, cotton and peanuts, whose stalks burnt better. The straw was used to feed cattle, which gave dung for burning.

Dung is a rather emotive material. It is basically South Asian fuel; the only other country where I have seen it burnt is Egypt, where they used to make dungcakes with a hole in the middle, and stacked them on poles at the corners of their huts. Foreigners—and sophisticated Indians—scoff at smelly dungcakes. More knowledgeable people also think that burning is a waste of dung which makes good organic manure. But there was an entire technology of dung utilization. Dung has a lot of inorganic material, and burns slowly; but you can make faster-burning variants by mixing straw with it. Straw used in walls can be sealed with dung; the straw acts as reinforcing, just as steel does in a modern building, and the dung is an excellent insulator. It makes a beautiful floor, firm enough to be swept every day, and cool to sit and sleep on. It is an excellent medium to paint on, as Warli folk artists of Maharashtra would tell you.

Anyway, Indian villagers had a lot of cattle, and a lot of sun to dry dung. Not all people across the world were so lucky; and they had more trouble collecting fuel for cooking as their population grew and forests receded. That is how mineral coal came to be used as domestic heating and cooking fuel. This happened in countries endowed with coal on the ground or not too deep underground—Britain, Germany, and more recently, China.

Then it was discovered in the eighteenth century that if coal was burnt with insufficient air, it gave out a gas—a mixture of methane and carbon monoxide—which could be burnt. British and German towns acquired gasworks from which gas was piped to homes. Our own Calcutta and Bombay had rudimentary gas supply systems. The great thing about gas was that it could be turned on and off just like water. Its heat output could therefore be controlled; it could deliver high heat for frying, low heat for simmering, or variable heat for an oven.

But coal gas required a lot of digging up of streets, laying of pipes, and their protection against leaks since it was the ideal medium for quick asphyxiation. It needed heavy investment and a continuous supply of coal. In the late nineteenth century, a substitute was discovered which was easier to mine and transport—mineral oil. Especially in the United States where oil was found close to the surface, the oil industry expanded rapidly, and homes changed over to kerosene. Kerosene was, however, expensive, and won markets only slowly. My mother, for instance, used a primus stove, where kerosene was pushed up into the wick with an air pump, for quick cooking such as making tea, a charcoal-burning shagri for normal cooking, and a firewood-burning boiler for bath water. The correct fuel mix was a matter of fine economic calculation.

At that time there was no electricity in villages; electricity was produced in power plants which, like gasworks, served the nearby towns. Villagers used hurricane lanterns—so called because with a metal dome and a glass chimney, they were not put off by rain or wind. Making hurricane lanterns was a major industry till the 1960s which entered the index of industrial production.

The lantern was the classic poor man's consumer durable; that is why the government started subsidizing kerosene. But already, kerosene was passing as an illuminant. In the 1950s, if one flew at night one could see villages dotted with the light of lanterns. (The airplanes of that time—mostly Dakotas—were propeller planes which flew quite low, at a height of about 3000 metres, below the cloud cover. So one sometimes got a bumpy ride if one hit air pockets; but in return one got a much better view of the ground.) But already by that time, battery cells were becoming cheap, villagers were changing over to torches which could be turned off and on at will, and lanterns were being used more selectively. Instead of watching moths try to sacrifice themselves to the unapproachable flame of lanterns, villagers began to listen to transistor radios. And rural electrification started in the late 1960s.

The politically correct view was, and still is, that kerosene is the favourite illuminant of the rural poor, and that electricity is provided to villages only for irrigation. But according to the National Council of Applied Economic Research, 19 per cent of rural families in 1995 had ceiling fans—that is, electricity as well as a roof sturdy enough to hold a fan. Table fans were in 13 per cent of the families. We do not know how many families had electricity; they could be a third to a half. They were certainly not using electricity only for irrigation; and if they had electric lights, they were unlikely to be using kerosene lanterns.

Everyone's preferred fuel is liquefied petroleum gas (LPG)—because its heat output can be so easily controlled. But LPG is subsidized—oil companies sell it below cost. This means that they like to sell as little of it as possible. Hence the scarcity, consumer registrations, authorized dealers, and the extreme difficulty of getting registered. Members of Parliament get 100 gas connections a year as a perk. The idea was to enable them to favour valuable constituents. But in 1993 it was discovered that they gave connections mostly to people outside their constituency. There was a thriving black market that their entitlement fed. So their privilege was abolished. The BJP government, in an effort to ingratiate itself with MPs, reintroduced the entitlement in 1998.

If a producer is forced to sell a product below cost, he will sell as little of it as possible, and there will be perpetual scarcity. Scarcity will raise the market price above the subsidized price; anyone who can get hold of gas at the subsidized price will make a profit by reselling. This is the recipe for a black market; in every urban neighbourhood in India, someone—a watchman, a shopkeeper, the gas dealer—can be found who will get you gas without your being entitled to it. This is how disrespect for rules is bred; but above all, less gas is sold to fewer people than if the gas subsidy were removed.

The same is the effect of the kerosene subsidy; oil companies sell as little as they can, there is a permanent scarcity, and a thriving black market. But here, the primary objective of the subsidy—to help poor villagers—is not met. For most of the ration-card holders are urban. They have electricity, and they use kerosene for cooking. Many of them use kerosene because they do not have the influence necessary for a gas registration. And kerosene is very similar to high-speed diesel oil, which was subsidized less (now it is not subsidized; but it bears a very low tax, so it is much cheaper than petrol). So kerosene is used to adulterate diesel oil and goes to ruin diesel engines.

Realizing the ill-effects of the subsidies, the government licensed private suppliers in 1993 to supply kerosene and gas without subsidy. But their market was very vulnerable to how much the government oil companies supplied with subsidy; whenever the subsidized supplies rose, the market for unsubsidized supplies shrank. The uncertainty and variability of demand ruined the business of the private licencees.

Every consumer likes subsidies, and resists their removal. But if subsidies are removed at the right time—for instance, if they had been removed in the last three years as world oil prices came down—their disappearance would hardly be noticed. What would be noticed, however, is the change in market. Shortages and black markets would disappear, kerosene and gas would become available in shops off-the-shelf, and their consumption would increase much faster, for the producers would have every incentive to sell as much as they could. We have quite forgotten that just ten years ago, if we wanted to build a house, we had to get a cement permit, and if it was not enough, buy cement in the black market. A.R. Antulay, when he was chief minister of Maharashtra, made a lot of money by selling cement permits. He was cautious enough to siphon it into a dummy institution called Indira Pratishthan, but he still had to resign.

There is far more natural gas discovered than there is oil; oil companies are sitting on huge reserves of it, and would love to find a market for it. If they are allowed, they would bring liquefied natural gas from Iran, Kuwait and Bahrain in huge refrigerated ships, unload it into pipelines and deliver it to homes all over India. But that will not happen for two reasons. First, the government-owned oil companies have an eye on this business, and they will do their best to keep competitors out. And they will not have enough money to expand supplies as fast as their competitors. And as long as gas and kerosene are subsidized, the market for unsubsidized gas will be too uncertain to attract private investors.

Diversity in food

If I have given the impression that advances in fuels and processes have been more important than a growing diversity of foods, it is deliberate. For food habits are tenacious. They change only slowly, and then under the force of circumstances—of demographic pressures, and of consequent changes in the availability of foods.

In fact, it is likely that over centuries, the range of foods eaten by major population groups narrowed. In the last chapter I talked about the diet of prehistoric populations—they ate a considerable range of wild animals, fruit, roots and vegetables that have today disappeared from the menus of their descendants. The rise in population density put a distance between people and foraging areas; people became increasingly dependent on eating what they produced.

Although collected foods declined as population became agricultural and sedentary, the land provided a variety of foods. The variety was greater where there was uncultivated land in the neighbourhood—mountains, forests, grasslands. It was also greater in the greener and more fertile areas; the closer one went to the deserts, the less the diversity.

But the diversity declined more drastically once urban, non-agricultural populations began to grow. That is when diets began to be dominated by mass produced foods. Thus, when the Europeans spread out to conquer the world, they carried preserved meat as their major food. Later, when industrial cities emerged in Britain, they were supplied by corn—wheat and maize—from the United States, and meat—mostly beef and lamb—from the US, Australia and New Zealand. The urban Japanese subsisted on fish caught by their fishing fleets, which ranged across the Pacific.

After World War II, a new trend has emerged—importing animal feedstuffs rather than meat. Thus the Netherlands imports oilseeds, mills them to extract oil, and feeds the oilcake to animals which it exports to Germany. It has such a huge business of meat exports that this small country is getting inundated with animal shit. It tried five years ago to sell manure to India; but the manure was very cheap, so farmers in Gujarat agitated and stopped the import.

In the past twenty years, the South-East Asian countries and China have begun to import oilcake, corn and coarse grains to feed animals. India has made good business out of this rising demand for oilcake in East Asia—and would have done even better if the government had not banned the import of oilseeds. Oil milling is a undemanding industry in terms of investment and technology, and Indian oil millers have considerable excess capacity. If they had been allowed, they would have imported oilseeds, milled them, sold the oil at home and exported the oilcake. But the government has prevented them from doing so in the name of protecting farmers.

Thus industrialization and urbanization have invariably led to dependence on a narrow range of mass-produced foods, chiefly grains, meat and fish. But this has begun to change in industrial countries since the 1970s. Trade barriers have fallen, transport costs have declined, and refrigeration techniques have improved. India has done very well out of the widespread love of cashewnuts in the West and Russia.

The Japanese for long remained wedded to their spartan, healthy diet. But because they exported so much and imported so little, whenever their officials met officials from the United States or Europe, they were widely harangued and abused for importing so little. As a result they had special promotions for Scotch whiskeys and French wines. Promotion of branded drinks is a strange business. My friend in Tokyo takes me to a bar which serves only Jim Beam whiskey. Every customer has his own bottle; it bears his name on an elegant silvery necklace. Whenever he comes—even after weeks or months—his personal bottle will be opened and drinks poured out exclusively for him and his friends. Conversation is thrown in; Japanese bartenders make it a point to chat to their customers and set them at ease. Haruki Tsuchiya takes me to this bar because it had an English-speaking hostess for me—a young woman who had escaped from China and come to study in Japan.

Drinks and cigarettes are amongst the most migratory products. Imperial Tobacco—now known as British American Tobacco—has an old brand called 555; it is the most smuggled brand in the world. Camel probably comes second. It is estimated that more cigarettes are smuggled into China than are consumed in India. Indians prefer whiskey when it comes to a taste for smuggled goods—or at least, used to until the manufacture of foreign brands was allowed in 1994. Scotch has become such a standard drink of the Indian upper class that it is difficult to imagine that 150 years ago it was virtually unknown. Our Muslim rulers were generally teetotallers; that is why we have such lovely non-alcoholic drinks like thandai and khus. The British in India mainly drank wine. Then, in 1868, a phyllora epidemic destroyed France's grape crop, and there was a famine of wine. The steel frame of the Indian Civil Service tottered. British officers were in agony, and had to call doctors. Their doctors, who were mostly Scottish, prescribed a peg of Scotch for their ailment. That is how our rulers changed over to Scotch, and the people followed.

Diversification of food and drinks has particularly accelerated in the past quarter century. It has much to do with the cheapening of air transport, improved refrigeration, and falling trade barriers. Grains and meat have been internationally traded for a long time. Till the mid-nineteenth century, meat used to be cured or smoked before being shipped; then refrigeration arrived. In the early years, refrigeration was pretty primitive. Proper temperature and humidity control came only after World

War II; the first test was the export of Caribbean bananas to Europe. Bananas are a very sensitive fruit; getting them to the consumers just ready to eat is quite an art. After the success of Caribbean bananas in Britain, our State Trading Corporation decided to venture; it sent a shipload of bananas to Russia. The whole load got spoilt, and the STC had to pay a lot to have the stinking ship cleaned. But elsewhere, preservation techniques have so improved that bananas in Berlin are crisper than in Kerala, and kiwi fruit from New Zealand and oranges from Israel have become items of mass consumption in Europe.

Industrialization of cooking

The last great difference between the American and Indian food habits is in the relative importance of home and factory as food processors. As people get rich, they eat more foods prepared by others; and more of those others are large businesses preparing food on a mass scale.

Cooking is a thermal and chemical process which can be reproduced on a large scale. But it continues to be a cottage industry in most of the world. The reason is twofold. Many populations are too scattered to offer a large enough concentrated market for processed foods. And people find it cheaper to prepare the foods themselves. The market value of their time is not high enough for them to go to work and to buy processed food with their earnings.

It is not a choice between entirely home-produced and entirely factory-produced food. The degree of outside processing can vary: for instance, green chana may be peeled before being sold, it may be dried and roasted to make a ready-to-eat snack, or it may be made into aalu chhole and sold in a restaurant. And a family may buy certain foods—for instance, sliced bread—entirely readymade, and make others—for instance, parathas for breakfast—entirely at home. The point is that in a richer society, the proportion of home labour in the food that is eaten will be lower.

As less is made at home and more is purchased outside, the market for processed foods also expands. Take ice cream. Kulfi, the Indian variant, goes back at least some centuries; it probably came from Iran. The Mughal kings were habitual users of ice. Some was made in the Ramlila ground just outside the fort of Shahjehanabad (old Delhi). On cold winter nights, water was allowed to trickle down reeds. Icicles formed on the reeds; they were scraped off, and blocks of ice were made. Ice was also transported on camels from Kashmir. The technique of kulfi-making has hardly changed from those times. But kulfi was a royal luxury.

Ice cream migrated down to the upper middle classes with the arrival of factory-produced ice. The ice was placed in a wooden bucket. There was a bar across the top of the bucket; through the top passed a spindle which could be turned with a handle at the top. The spindle held a container full of sweetened milk with pistachios, almonds and other titbits. Children of the house took turns rotating the spindle. As the container went round and round, the milk chilled. After hours of child labour, the milk turned solid; it was then scooped out. This technique, which probably arose in English households in the nineteenth century, was still in use in my childhood. The ice cream it made was more grainy than the oversmooth industrial product we get today. Just a decade ago I saw ice cream being made the old way in a very popular ice cream shop in Ottawa—except that the spindle was turned by an electric motor.

Ice factories sprang up all over the country with the advent of electricity; and where there was ice, there was ice cream. But ice cream remained a cottage industry; every town had an ice cream factory, and some had many. Often it was an adjunct of a restaurant chain. That is how the Kwality ice creams started, for serving in Kwality restaurants which were renowned for their food in the 1950s. But eventually the Wig family's ice cream business far outgrew its restaurant business, and spread all over India. In 1993 the ice cream business was sold to Hindustan Lever.

The story of cold drinks is similar. Bottled drinks were first made to dilute alcoholic drinks. Whiskey was diluted with soda water, which was water in which some carbon dioxide was imprisoned to give it a slight tangy taste; the carbon dioxide also acted as a mild antacid. Similarly, gin was diluted with tonic water, which was water mixed with sugar and a tiny pinch of quinine to keep malaria away; the tonic sold by Schweppes in Britain is still called India tonic water. The range was extended with orange and lemon-flavoured drinks. The bottles of all these drinks were closed by a glass marble inside the bottle; since the bottles contained carbon dioxide injected under pressure, it pushed up the marble into the mouth of the bottle and kept it closed. The bottle had a wire device on top which could be used to push down the marble and release the drink. The cold drink industry was also a local one; every town had its own brands of cold drinks.

Then came Coca-Cola in the 1950s; in the next twenty years, it took over an increasing share of the market, while the little local cold drink works closed down or became franchisees of Coca-Cola. The invasion of Coca-Cola caused much emotion. I remember once going to interview C. Subramaniam in the late sixties on television. It was a blazing hot day, made worse by the arc lights. The producer offered a Coke to Subramaniam, who snorted, 'Coca-Cola? I never drink Coca-Cola!' So I asked for one myself. That was a suitably icy beginning to a hot interview. Ten years later, George Fernandes became industry minister and threw Coca-Cola out of India with great fanfare. Then in the mid-1980s, Pepsi came in with Rajiv Gandhi's permission, and in the 1990s, Coca-Cola returned. One of the biggest beneficiaries of the exit of Coca-Cola was Ramesh Chauhan of Parle, who had his own cola drink in the market; he threw as many hurdles as he could to the entry of Pepsi and later Coca-Cola. Finally in 1993 he sold out his business to Coca-Cola, and became its franchisee. He benefited from its re-entry too; Coca-Cola bought up his business for over Rs 1 billion.

Ice cream and cold drinks are instances of industries where a large number of small producers have given way to just one or two giants; and these giants are foreign companies. Both these facts evoke stormy passions. First, they have created monopolies or something close, and monopolies have a terrible reputation in economics; it is supposed to be in their nature to fleece customers. Second, they are foreign, and evoke fears of another foreign takeover of the economy.

The first fear is easier to address. A monopoly can make superprofits in an industry which produces something that people have no substitute for; and Coca-Cola or ice cream are not such products. There are plenty of substitutes for Coca-Cola, quite apart from Pepsi. Anyone can make up a cold drink at home; and if Coke becomes very expensive, anyone can set up a cold drink factory. It is an industry that is easy to enter; and that is what limits profits. The same is true of ice cream. Industrial countries have much more concentrated ice cream industries; for instance, Walls in England and Baskin Robbins in the US. But local ice cream shops keep cropping up, which give homemade flavours impossible for mass factories to emulate. What matters is not how many producers there are in any industry, but whether it is easy to enter the industry, how dispensable its products are, and whether there are other producers producing close substitutes. The question to ask is not how many producers there are, but whether there are signs of extraordinary profits. There usually are not in consumer goods industries with few players.

The fear of foreign domination has much to do with the way the government views the world. There are governments which harbour terrible suspicions of other governments, and governments which are relaxed about it. International hostility was more fashionable as long as the cold war was on. Most countries took sides, as did India, and were paranoid about the other side. With the collapse of the Soviet Union, international confrontations have also subsided. There still are countries in perpetual hostility towards some country or another, such as North Korea, or Iraq; there is also the United States which has the capacity and the willingness to initiate or participate in hostilities far away from its shores. These countries will have strong views about foreign enterprises operating on their soil or their own enterprises operating abroad.

The Indian government also used to have such strong views because we were involved on the weaker side in the cold war; and the cold war fears persist, though they have weakened. In contrast to India, the Chinese government believes that it is strong enough to defend its interests, and that all enterprises on Chinese soil, foreign or Chinese, create production and employment and are storehouses of skills. The Chinese welcome to foreign enterprises has brought it enormous quantities of foreign investment and helped make it an economic powerhouse. Conversely,

Indian misgivings make for unpredictable shifts in its policies towards foreign investment, and give foreign companies the impression that these policy shifts make India a risky country to do business in; they cannot forget that George Fernandes is still around. This perception of government risk has put off foreign investors. Indian political parties associate risk with foreign investment, and foreign companies associate risk with the Indian political system. Each finds support for its fears in the behaviour of the other.

But independently of foreign companies, the process of industrialization of food and of emergence of large food product companies continues. Haldiram is emerging as a large supplier of snacks which once were made at home. Flour is also becoming available in branded packs. These things are happening without involvement of foreign companies; they are just a reflection of the fact that as Indians get richer, they buy food products instead of making them.

SHELTER

According to table 2, the average American consumption of food is seven times the Indian consumption. As we saw, this difference is largely due to differences in the range of foods consumed, cooking services bought in the form of processed foods, and ease of cooking; differences in physical quantities eaten account for little. Food has a large element of habit; many Indians would prefer their own food just as many Americans would prefer their own. To each his own poison.

But the Indian consumption of housing, in the form of rent, was only 3 per cent of the US level. This strikes a chord, for there is hardly any country in the world where so many people are so poorly housed as in India, and few countries where they are as well housed as in the United States. Property is expensive in India; the UN cost of living indexes place Bombay and Delhi housing as among the most expensive in the world. And it is not cheap elsewhere in India; comparable property in comparable towns is cheaper in absolute terms in the US than in India. Most Indians would place problems related to housing—the cost, quality, size—high amongst their worries. A house is supposed to be a convenience to protect one from the extremes of heat and cold, hail and storm; but it is an inconvenience for so many of us. Why have we managed housing so badly in this country?

Whether it is a convenience or not, a house is above all a convention—a device for marking territory. There is the old cliché that an Englishman's home is his castle. What it meant was that an Englishman had a legal right to privacy; no one could invade his private space, not even the King's troops could enter a home without a proper warrant. An igloo is not a very convenient form of abode; for one thing, it is made of ice, so it cannot give great protection against the Arctic cold. Its crucial characteristic is that its orifice is too narrow for the polar bear; it tells the bear in language it would understand that the space is private.

Hence wherever there are houses, there have to be laws or conventions which define who may occupy a house, how a house may be acquired and disposed of, and in what conditions an occupant may be dispossessed. A house occupies physical space, and is usually stationary; the French aptly call property *immobilier.* Banjaras carry their huts in specially crafted bullock carts; and families in the West sometimes go on holiday in caravans attached to their cars. But these are exceptions; most houses get stuck for their lives wherever they are built; and they usually last very long.

So here is the landscape covered with houses, and here is the population milling around on the land. How are the two married together? How does the mobile population attach itself to the immobile houses? Without conventions it would become a game of musical chairs; when one goes to the office in the morning one would not know where one would be sleeping tonight. That would be inconvenient.

The commonest convention is that of property—that all real estate belongs to someone, who can transfer it to others by sale or gift. Such a rule requires a government to enforce it. What is there to prevent a person from selling property that is not his own, or selling it to a number of persons and decamping with the money? To prevent such frauds, it is necessary to have a record of property, which is modified only when legally binding sales take place. There can be only one such record, which the government must maintain.

Next, it would be useless to have a house if one could not get into or out of it; there has to be public access to it. In the countryside this can cause endless problems, for no one laid out streets before dividing up the land into fields. But there are customary rules about the right of access through others' fields. In the towns, however, the right of access is ensured by requiring that building needs prior permission from the government. At that point the approving authority ensures that the property can be accessed along a public road; this road would also carry power and telephone, and water pipes. Thus there has to be something like public property which surrounds all private property.

Third, the owner of a property may not reside in it. If

he rents or leases it, the relationship of the owner and tenant will be governed by a contract between them. But if there is no contract, one must be imputed; if there is a dispute, the contract must be interpreted or supplemented. This too is a service to be provided by the government.

Finally, the rules that give private owners exclusive use of their property cannot apply to government property; the public must have free access to roads, for instance. But they cannot set up houses on roads. Thus there has to be a law on the use of public property which is different from the law of private property.

In all these ways, the government will be involved in governing property and housing; and the laws it makes and the way it enforces them will affect the quality of housing a people get.

Land conversion

Houses must be built on land that was earlier put to some other use. In Japan, 85 per cent of the land is hilly; the government is determined to keep it forested. So the land available for housing is limited. It is confined to the coastal strip, where housing competes with agriculture for land space. On the west coast, the mountains are too close to the sea and leave little space for settlements. So most of the population is settled in a strip along the east coast, which is so narrow that from most places you can see the mountains to the west, and often the sea to the right.

Japan, like France and Britain, has a rather romantic view of farming. It tries to preserve the rural way of life, and to persuade the few farmers who are kind enough to continue farming. The farmer is lucky he has a house to sleep in. His salaryman neighbour has had to work late in his office and is too late to come back home, so he goes to a cheap hotel. He does not get a room there, he gets a bunk; someone else is renting the bunk below one. Early in Japan's industrialization, workers could not afford houses, so employers housed them—chiefly unmarried girls earning pin money before marrying—in dormitories.

To ease the housing shortage, the Japanese government improved railway services after the War. Japan has the fastest trains in the world (except perhaps for France); suburban trains fan out across the cities, and are so punctual that you can set your watch by them. Timetables give the minutes between stations; even if you miss the names of stations, you can get down at the right station by counting minutes. This fantastic train service enables people to commute to work from as far away as 200 kilometres. There was some time, after World War II, when commuter trains were so crowded that the railways used to employ sturdy young men to cram passengers into the bogies before the doors closed.

With this improvement in train services, an increasing proportion of urban workers began to live in what were once rural communities. The distinction between town and country disappeared. While a salaryman—as the Japanese call their white collar workers—goes to town, his wife may go and grow vegetables in a plot close to her house; a farmer may go and work in the town, and come back in the evening to feed his fish or run a power tiller over his tiny farm. Villages have become urbanized; the process of converting rural into urban land has been obviated. Although Japanese houses continue to be small, a surprisingly high proportion of Japanese live in low-rise, often independent houses, in or close to the countryside.

Contrast this with the United States. The US has enormous amounts of flat land that can be urbanized. Conversion of rural land into townships requires permission, because the urban municipality would have to provide services. But the government does not have to intervene in the urbanization of rural land. American farms are large. A builder who wants to build a township—a development as they call it—has only to negotiate with a small number of farmers and buy the land. He typically divides the land into plots, lays down the roads and utilities, and connects the township to the adjoining city. The city corporation approves the plans before building begins; at that point it ensures that the public areas and facilities are adequate. The entire process of converting rural into urban land, which causes so much vexation elsewhere, is trouble-free.

While the Japanese travel in trains, the Americans drive cars. The US government has made considerable investments in roads, and the Americans are habitual car owners. Since roads can reach more places than railways, the resulting settlement patterns are less concentrated. Much traffic moves in Japan along a north-south ribbon. In the US, traffic moves all over.

Also, since the infrastructure—power, water, communications—is equally good all over the country, businesses spread out; less activity and less population are concentrated in megacities than it is in Japan and Europe.

Hence not only are land prices lower in the US, the price pyramids have lower peaks. Land prices tend to form pyramids: they are highest in city centres which house the most profitable businesses, and go down as one goes away from the city centres. Just about a decade ago, when Japan was still booming, the market value of the land in Tokyo exceeded the value of all the land in the United States. What this meant was that the price pyramid in Tokyo was very tall.

India faces no physical shortage of urbanizable land

like Japan. As in the US, India's towns are surrounded by plenty of land on which towns can spread out. But private developers cannot extend the cities here in the same way as they do in the US. For the holdings that surround towns in India are tiny by US standards. A developer who wants to set up a township would have to buy land from a very large number of owners. He would have to negotiate with each to buy his land; each would look at the builder with his own combination of greed and suspicion, each would expect a different price, and some would not sell at any price. If one of the last has land right in the middle of the area, the builder would not be able to develop the area at all.

Hence compulsion is used in India; the government buys up land by force for urban expansion. For this purpose, the state governments have set up urban development authorities. They buy up land at what is defined by law as a fair price. However, these authorities do not simply acquire the land and pass it on to builders; they hoard the land, and develop the land themselves—divide it up and lay down roads, water, sewage, communications etc.—and then sell the plots. They generally do not sell the plots to builders; instead, they sell to the ultimate owners—house-owners, housing cooperatives, factory-owners and so on. The idea is to deprive middlemen—builders, estate agents, finance companies—of the profits of urban development, and instead to pass these on to more deserving members of the society like industrialists, artists, poor people and so on. Urban development is nationalized for the public good.

That is the theory. But the results are very different. The difference between the price of rural and urban land indicates how much profit is to be made out of urban development; it is huge. But this profit never shows in the accounts of the urban development authorities. The prices at which they buy are 'fair' in law, but they are so low as to generate considerable resistance from the farmers who lose their land. So the process of land acquisition is extremely slow. Once they have acquired the land, the authorities are in no hurry to sell it off; they think that the longer they sit on the land, the more valuable it will become. Since they would not sell to middlemen, they cannot sell the land by auction where anyone may buy it.

This has four consequences. First, they get a lower price than they would from an auction. Second, the restrictions they place on who may buy create a web of deceit. For instance, the restriction that a buyer may own only one property; many owners of multiple properties simply lie and get more properties. Third, the politicians and bureaucrats who control the authorities buy up a disproportionate part of the properties in their own names, or in the names of relatives and friends, or in bogus names. Often, parties or governments make politicians and bureaucrats declare their assets; sometimes, the more corrupt of them are investigated, and investigating agencies release lists of their assets. It is remarkable how important property is in the assets of such bureaucrats and politicians—how insignificant shares and bonds are in comparison. The reason is that capturing the profits of compulsorily acquired land is a major source of the profits of those in power. And finally, where superiors are corrupt, subordinates get a licence to be corrupt. In every activity of the authority—contracts for construction, utility works, allocation of plots—corruption creeps in.

And the profits of urban development seep out; the authorities never earn a commercial return on the investments they make in land acquisition and development. Since they do not earn enough, they cannot borrow to finance their activities; they are therefore thrown upon the resources of the state governments. The state governments are short of money for the same reasons as the authorities. That is how urban development authorities simply cannot develop enough land to meet the needs of the growing urban populations.

Because the urban development authorities cannot cope with demand, land gets converted to urban use without their intervention. People employed in towns begin renting rooms or buying housing in surrounding villages. Village grocers begin to stock shampoos for their new urban clients. Buses begin clattering between the villages and the metropolis. Because the state governments have eliminated private enterprise from urban development, India is going the Japanese way: villages are getting urbanized. The only difference is that the Japanese government upgraded their infrastructure—roads, power, water and communications—as they became part of the cities, whereas the governments in India cannot do so. That is why these urban villages come to fester without sewage, to have substandard power supply and telephone lines, and their roads become clogged with traffic. If the urban development authorities gave up the unrealistic aim of housing for all, they might be better able to ensure roads and water for all.

Only one experiment promises to be different. The Maharashtra government wanted to take over villages in Khed taluk near Pune and develop the land for factories. It just happened that Sharad Joshi, the farmers' leader, lives in Ambethan village in this taluk. He persuaded the government to allow the farmers to form a company to develop the land. The farmers would give their land to the company and get shares in it. The company would develop the land and lease it to factories; it would pay farmers a dividend from the income. Instead of having to sell the land to Maharashtra Housing and Development Authority, the farmers would keep the land; instead of MHADA, the farmers would earn any rise in the price of the land; instead of one-time compensation, they would get an income as long as they keep their shares in the company.

Land allocation

Conversion of unbuilt into built land requires government intervention because villagers and land developers will not otherwise be able to arrive quickly at satisfactory bargains. The government solves this problem by forcing villagers to sell land to itself and by monopolizing land development; but this government operation is so riddled with leakages that it never manages to convert enough land.

As land gets converted to urban use, it also gets allocated to various uses. Land gets covered with buildings; those buildings and their occupants determine how the land is used. This conversion must match the uses for which land is being demanded. There are millions of people wanting houses, offices or factories, and there is only so much unbuilt land. There has to be some mechanism to connect the two.

It would be wonderful if everyone who wanted to use land had the cash to buy it. In fact, very few do. Houses are so expensive that people cannot buy them outright. Some industrialists may be rich enough to buy land outright; but even they would find it easier to set up industry if they did not have to pay the full price on the spot. Many more people would be able to afford accommodation, whether for living or for some activity like an office or factory, if they could rent it.

Before someone can rent a house, it is necessary that

someone else should be prepared to build or buy a house for renting. And since most of the population cannot buy a house, a small number of landlords must be prepared to invest in a lot of houses for renting. In other words, for the mass of the population to be housed, there must be an industry, or a small class of landlords, who specialize in renting houses.

People will go into the profession of owning houses for renting only if they can be sure of getting the rent. But what if someone moves into a house and refuses to pay rent? Then the landlord could force him to vacate the house. He could employ ruffians to do it. But that would bring a class of ruffians into the picture; and they are not going to sit around waiting for landlords to come and commission them for an expulsion job. They will find work for themselves, and that will be uncomfortable for many innocent people. It is better if the expulsion is done by the government in strictly controlled circumstances, subject to law and contract. There should be an agreement between the landlord and tenant, there should be laws about what agreements are enforceable and which are not, and there should be a monopolist of force who would apply it when the agreement is broken.

It sounds terrible that the monopolist of force—which is another name for government—should go about expelling tenants in trouble with their landlords. But that is the best way of ensuring that people build houses for others to live in. There would not be enough houses for tenants to live in unless landlords could expect them to pay rent or leave the house—or be compelled to leave.

This kind of paradox is to be found in many situations where trust is involved: more money will be given, and more assets built on trust, if breach of trust attracts sure and swift punishment. For instance, people have become very wary of investing in company shares in the past four years. It is because they invested in many companies in 1992-96 which never paid any dividends, and which often vanished without a trace. If there had been sure and swift punishment for embezzling money, trust in company managements would not have been lost so completely.

Something happened in India half a century ago that destroyed the trust that a defaulting tenant would be forced to leave the house; that loss of trust is one reason for the high rents and the difficulty in getting rented accommodation. What happened was World War II. At that time, India became the staging point for the war against the Japanese. Thousands of allied troops landed up in India, and had to be billeted. Their officers had to be found swank accommodation. The massive expenditure on war created jobs for government accountants, procurement officers, railway officials and many others. For all these bureaucrats there were not enough houses. So the government 'requisitioned' houses—that is, it took over vacant houses and fixed 'controlled' rents for them. As the war progressed, prices rose, and these controlled rents became ever more inadequate. The lower they fell in relation to uncontrolled rents, the more people wanted government accommodation. And since it was so unfair that government employees should pay low controlled rents while others paid much more, the government introduced controls on private rents as well. As the rents remained low while construction costs rose, it soon became unprofitable to build houses for renting. That is how the scarcity of rental accommodation developed.

As time went by, the government realized the folly of rent control, and relaxed it. The relaxation was slow and halting—after all, we had democratic governments and there are always more tenants than landlords. First, rent control was relaxed if the rent was above a certain amount; then it was relaxed on new construction. But even the relaxation was unjust as between those whose rents were controlled and those whose rents were not. So many cases ended up in courts. Courts were overburdened with rent control cases, and took years to decide a case. Hence the relaxation did not assure landlords of a swift and sure resolution to a dispute with a tenant.

This lack of assurance affected different tenants differently. Thus, big companies were considered less likely to renege on tenancy agreements. So people were more prepared to build offices than houses. Foreigners, especially from the rich countries like the US, Europe and Japan—were considered more likely to pay rent and to vacate houses. So it was—and is—much easier for them to get houses than for home-grown tenants. Among home-grown tenants, those from far away were considered more honest than one's own kind. Thus in Delhi, a Punjabi landlord would prefer a South Indian tenant to a fellow-Punjabi; the converse held true in Madras.

The worst affected were the poor; they were considered the most likely to default, and the rent they paid was so low that it would be less worthwhile to sue them. Hence landlords simply stopped building for the poor. But every city generates more jobs for the poor than for the rich; and if they work, they are going to live somewhere. So they squatted wherever they could—on government land, in forests, along railway lines, along open sewers and so on. They were too many to remove; most of them got votes, and used them to protect their encroachment, and to get basic facilities like water and power. But they were not given permanent occupation of the land; the authorities that owned the land reserved the right to eject them. This is how Indian cities came to be the slummiest and shabbiest in the world. The only other country where I have seen equally impressive slums is Brazil; and even there the poor live in better houses, because they have been allowed to improve the houses. In Bombay, there is a ban on slum dwellers building houses over fourteen feet high. Elsewhere, their huts can be demolished at any time, and are not worth building in any style.

Land and lending

I have just mentioned phantom companies, which were floated, collected money from shareholders and disappeared. Those who take shares are legally part-owners of a company. They get a share of the company's profits in the form of a dividend; the dividend is decided by the directors. Shareholders never get their investment back unless their company is liquidated, its assets sold off, and its debts paid off; what remains is then shared out between the shareholders in proportion to their investment. But as long as the company is running, they cannot get their capital back—unless they sell their shares to someone.

A houseowner never gives his house to a tenant on such terms: he never says, 'Pay me a share if you make a good profit, otherwise you don't have to pay me anything.' He always contracts to pay a fixed rent, which may be revised—generally upwards—every once in a while. So income from rent is very stable.

So it would make sense for someone who wants to rent out property to borrow money for it and promise to pay a fixed interest on the loan; the rent would cover the interest. For a lender too, it is a very safe loan, for against it stands a solid building. To give the lender additional comfort, the landlord may promise that if he fails to repay the loan, the lender may take over the property and sell it to recover his money; this kind of title on property is a mortgage. Property and mortgage loans feed upon each other; countries where mortgage lending is well developed are better housed, and countries with large property markets have large mortgage business. Many governments encourage mortgage lending institutions by giving tax concessions to mortgage borrowers; as a result, specialist mortgage banks have emerged in some countries. They are called building societies in Britain and savings-and-loan associations in the US.

Buildings are expensive and require large loans to finance; hence the repayment of the loans is spread out over many years—seldom less than ten, going up to thirty or more. Banks that give such long loans tend to specialize in them; to finance them they try to attract long-term deposits, and they develop special expertise in judging property and title.

If someone can borrow to buy a house and rent it out, he can also buy the house for himself. Instead of paying rent to a landlord, he would pay a monthly instalment to the mortgage lender. If he continues to pay the instalment for many years, he may finish paying, and may find himself master of his house with no more to pay. That is the dream of many a young couple; as soon as possible they find a house, buy it with a mortgage loan, and settle down to pay for it. Mortgage banks themselves encourage it since young people have many years of earnings ahead of them.

But to protect themselves in case the borrower defaults or the price of the property falls, they give loans for only a part of its price—seldom more than 90 per cent; often the higher this part, the higher the interest rate. For young people, even the 10 to 20 per cent they have to put in is often too high. To turn such people into clients, mortgage banks encourage them to start building up their equity—that is, their contribution towards the cost of the house—by saving and depositing the money with the banks. Some mortgage banks are mutual societies; they treat depositors like shareholders, and give them a part of the banks' profits. In this way, they try to inveigle young people into a long-term relationship with them. The blandishments often succeed; young people take on as large a mortgage as they can afford on their income, and move into expensive family homes expecting to stay indebted for most of their lives. A couple in their forties I knew moved into an eighteenth century cottage with an enclosed garden in a prime area of south London. The property was quite beyond their ability to pay, and they fully expected to leave it to the building society when they died; in their lifetimes, however, they would live in style.

However, whereas the rent is fixed as long as the rental agreement lasts, the payments on the mortgage are not. The part that depends on the loan taken does not vary; but the interest burden varies with the interest rates at which the mortgage bank can borrow, and hence with the market rate of interest. So if the interest rate goes up, the bank may well ask you to pay a bigger monthly instalment. Those who have borrowed to the hilt to live well may suddenly find the instalment rising above their capacity to pay.

But there is a still bigger danger for mortgage borrowers. At higher interest rates, mortgage loans cost more, fewer people can afford them, and the demand for houses is less. Hence the prices of houses will also go down. A house can be regarded as a marketable asset that yields a certain income stream in the form of rent. There are other such assets; for instance, a government bond or company debenture can be sold in the stock exchange and bring a stream in the form of interest. The price of such a security is just the interest it yields divided by the market rate of interest. In the same way, the price of houses goes up and down inversely with the market rate of interest.

Now remember that when a mortgage bank gives a loan on a house, the loan covers only a part—60 to 90 per cent—of the cost of the house; the rest has to be found by the buyer. The difference between the cost of the house and the loan is called the owner's equity. If the price of the house falls enough, it will fall below the loan taken on it. If at that point the owner defaults on the loan and walks away leaving the house to the mortgage bank, the bank will not be able to cover its loan by selling the house. The owner's equity will be negative; and a bank does not like that. So as prices fall and the owner's equity shrinks, the mortgage bank will ask the owner to bring in more equity. If a young couple has borrowed to the hilt to buy its dream house, they may not be able to cough up the additional cash. They may have to get out of the house and on the street, together with the baby and the little dog.

Thus big rises in interest rates can cause a social upheaval in a nation with a well-developed mortgage market. This is what happened in the United States after the Latin American debt crisis in the late 1970s. Interest rates went up, mortgage instalments were raised, many borrowers could not pay, properties were sold dirt cheap, savings and loan associations made losses and went bankrupt. The government had to liquidate many of them and rescue some which were not so badly off.

A similar crisis occurred in Britain later in the 1980s. The British pound was tied to other European currencies in an arrangement called the Snake: the Bank of England could not allow its exchange rate with the German mark and the French franc from going above or below a certain limit. The British balance of payments was adverse, and investors did not believe that the Bank of England could keep the pound in the Snake. To persuade them to leave their money in Britain, the Bank of England kept the interest rates high, and bankrupted many a householder. In April 1993, the Indian finance minister Manmohan Singh was in London and had been invited to lunch by Norman Lamont, the British Chancellor of the Exchequer. Uncharacteristically, he was late; his private secretary kept going up to Manmohan Singh every few minutes and apologizing: the Chancellor of the Exchequer, he said, was delayed in Parliament and would be there in a minute. He never did; that day he devalued the pound. Then the Bank of England could bring down the interest rates and save the common British house-owner.

Thus if a nation is to become a property-owning and debt-owing democracy, it helps if its interest rates are low and steady. Keeping them so is a trick that few countries manage. But it is worth trying if a nation wants to be well housed.

There are two conditions it must fulfil if it wants to keep its interest rates low. The first is that its balance of payments must be strong: on balance it should be earning more foreign exchange than it is spending, investing abroad or reducing its foreign liabilities. Britain in the latter half of the nineteenth century had a strong balance of payments because of the huge income it was getting from all its investments abroad—in the US, in Latin America, in India and Africa. So its interest rates were low; that was the long period of low interest rates when its building societies flourished and Britain became a nation of debtors. Switzerland in the latter part of the twentieth century was another such country. The rich people of the world parked their money in Swiss banks; the inflow of their money kept the Swiss franc strong, and the interest rates low. There was even a time when current account holders had to pay Swiss banks interest to persuade the banks to hold their money.

Further, a country must have low inflation if it is to have low interest rates. Savers will want at least to maintain the value of their savings if they are going to lend the money; that means that the interest rate they get must be higher than the rate of inflation. When I went to Argentina in 1990, inflation was running at a few hundred per cent a year. Petrol pumps had notices saying 'Sorry, no credit!' Banks had notices saying, 'Interest 40 per cent per month on deposits under 1 million pesos; for higher amounts, see the manager.' In Japan, on the other hand, prices are virtually stable, and mortgages can be had at 5 per cent. In Europe and the US, inflation is 2-3 per cent, and mortgages start from 8 per cent upwards.

India's balance of payments is weak; India imports more goods and services than it exports, and the deficit has to be bridged by attracting capital from abroad. And inflation in India is higher than in industrial countries; it has averaged 7 per cent over decades. And the costs of Indian financial institutions are high; they need a generous spread between their borrowing and lending rates. For all these reasons, interest rates in India are high, mortgage loans are expensive, and the housing they finance is limited. No wonder housing is so limited and expensive.

CONSUMER DURABLES

When people think of the Americans' superior standard of living, they think of consumer durables—of their big cars, and all the modern conveniences at home—dishwashers, vacuum cleaners, televisions with 50-inch screens and so on. And this impression is accurate; there is hardly any consumer durable of which American consumption per head was less than 200 times that in India in 1973.

Since then things have been changing in India as well; the purchases of consumer durables have been rising apace, as table 3 shows. In the ten years up to 1995-96, the proportion of households owning most consumer durables at least tripled; and some consumer durables such as washing machines, which were virtually unknown, have now entered Indian households.

Consumer durables serve various purposes; I would divide them into four types. First, there are vehicles. People cannot avoid travelling long distances in the modern urban society, and mechanical aids to do so are among the first durables to be acquired. Next, there are the classical consumer durables—the devices that save work. Then there are consumer durables which are not strictly necessary, but which it is convenient to possess. Finally, there are consumer goods which make our lives more comfortable or enjoyable.

Iron horses

The horse has virtually disappeared from the scene, especially in urban India; but it remains the standard of mobility. There was a time, some four thousand years ago, when there were no horses in India; none were traced in the Indus civilization. On the other hand, horses were very important in all ancient Aryan civilizations, and figure a lot in their lore, myth and religion. So do they also in Vedic and early Sanskrit literature; the name Ashwin literally means the horseman. There is now a vocal school of Indian historians who believe the Aryans were indigenous

TABLE 3

Number of consumer durables owned per 100 household

	1985-86	1995-96				
	Total	*Total*	*Poor*	*Not so poor*	*Middle*	*Not so rich*
Iron horses						
Bicycles	32	52	40	62	64	59
Scooters	2	6	1	4	15	26
Motor cycles	1	3	0	2	6	13
Mopeds	1	3	1	4	8	9
Work savers						
Mixer-grinders	3	11	2	10	26	40
Sewing machines	9	10	5	11	17	21
Washing machines	0	3	0	1	6	18
Conveniences						
Irons	7	16	5	19	32	45
Instant geysers	0	1	0	0	1	5

	1985-86	1995-96				
	Total	*Total*	*Poor*	*Not so poor*	*Middle*	*Not so rich*
Storage geysers	0	1	0	0	2	5
Pressure cookers	11	25	8	30	49	67
Mechanical watches	46	82	60	93	112	122
Quartz watches	9	38	36	41	67	102
Comforters						
Ceiling fans	21	37	13	41	70	100
Table fans	10	18	8	22	30	35
Refrigerators	3	9	1	5	20	44
Radios	16	43	33	53	53	50
Black & White TVs	5	24	11	35	41	35
Colour TVs	1	8	1	5	18	35

From I Natarajan, India Market Demographics Report 1998, National Council of Applied Economic Research, New Delhi, 1999.

to India; the horse remains the major obstacle to their belief.

The pulling power of the first locomotives was measured in the number of horse-equivalents; the power of cars is still so measured. The first trams in Europe were pulled by sturdy horses. There are still some horse carriages left in Bombay; they carry tourists along Marine Drive in the evenings. They are called Victorias; they were the rich man's Mercedes in Bombay in the late nineteenth century.

But already by then, the age of the horse was passing. The reason was the growth of cities. By the early nineteenth century, the major European cities—London, Hamburg, Amsterdam—were growing to a size which made the horse a serious traffic bottleneck. Horses could not travel faster than twelve miles an hour even on uncluttered roads; nor could they pull more than half a dozen passengers. The Europeans bred special horses for heavy draft; such horses were used to pull the first buses. But even such buses could not carry more than a couple of dozen passengers. As a result, roads were cluttered with carriages; and carriages competed for space with human beings, who did much miscellaneous walking, carrying and fetching. The chaotic clutter on the roads of that time is graphically described in the novels of Charles Dickens.

The first mechanical horse that came to assistance was the railway, which was first tried out in 1825; once it was proved practicable, the railway spread rapidly. But it was a very different animal from a horse. For one thing, it required a special, expensive track. To save on investment, other traffic had to be concentrated along railway tracks. Thus railways fanned out of towns; settlements emerged and fattened along the tracks. Medieval cities were more or less bulbous in shape—often round, sometimes with four or more sides. City walls were expensive to build, so they enclosed a broadly circular or elliptical area, and the inside was filled up with palaces, hovels and alleys. But with the advent of the railway, cities began to take the star shape familiar today. It was impossible to insert tracks into the towns of that time; so railway stations were built on the outskirts. Thus London has six 'termini' where railway lines ended—Paddington, Euston, King's Cross, Liverpool Street, Waterloo and Victoria. Bombay, Delhi, Calcutta and Madras all have two each.

Thus the early railways did not solve the problem of travel within the cities; on the contrary, they added to it, for passengers travelling through the city had to go from one railway station to another. And yet, the railway was the only technology available till almost the end of the nineteenth century to deal with with rising traffic density within towns. Steam buses made their appearance soon after the railways; but they needed to be replenished with coal and water three or four times a day.

The only way to use trains within cities was two-storied roads, one carrying animal-borne traffic and another a railway track. This is why the cities that expanded in that age—London, Paris, Berlin, New York—have underground local railways. Buenos Aires belongs to this select group; it reached the pinnacle of prosperity in the late nineteenth century by exporting beef to Britain, and the British built for it a metro railway which is almost a replica of the London underground.

Underground railways were marvels of engineering. They were generally built by the cut-and-fill method: a road was dug up, a waterproof steel tube was laid underneath it, and then it was filled up again. Tunnelling was generally impracticable unless there was hard rock underneath; cutting through rock was more expensive.

But underground railways took ages to build; the only

such line in India, in Calcutta, is quite short, but took fourteen years to build. And in the meanwhile, roads were in a mess, there were enormous hills of mud all along, and many houses developed cracks.

Even after the early underground trains started running, they created another kind of mess, for they ran on steam. They filled the tunnels with smoke; special ventilation shafts had to be made, and smoke had to be evacuated. The Japanese had a better solution: they placed their suburban trains on an additional storey built on top of the roads in Tokyo. This became possible because by the time they built their metro, in the 1920s and 1930s, steel had become cheaper and its quality had improved. The local government in Delhi is thinking of the same solution—of a metro on top of its Ring Road. But the Ring Road has in the meanwhile been cluttered with flyovers which trains cannot fly over, so a metro is going to require considerable reorganization of road traffic.

These problems ended only towards the end of the nineteenth century, when electricity could be applied to trains. But the early motors were not nearly as powerful as steam engines. Hence they found a new use. Tramways came to be built on existing roads. They reduced the space for other traffic since they required their own tracks; hence they could run only along broad highways which could accommodate both trams and road traffic. The frequent crossing of tram lines and roads made things difficult for everyone. But at last a medium of mass transport within the cities had arrived. Once trams began to run, the rate of growth of major cities accelerated.

Still, the railway era never saw a good solution to urban traffic problems. Collective transport was required for moving the masses, and a way could not be found of moving them along existing roads. The rich did not like the trains and trams, and stuck to their landaus and broughams; horse carriages continued to compete for road space, and clutter and dirty it.

The internal combustion engine finally removed the clutter; but it took a long time to offer a neat solution. The first problem was the fuel. In an external combustion engine—for instance, a steam engine—fuel is burnt in an open chamber with air, and heats water in a closed chamber; the water evaporates and turns into steam, the steam exerts increasing pressure as it heats up, and the pressure drives a shaft. Old people may remember the steam engines of Indian railways. The stoker kept shovelling coal into the fire box. The fire created hot steam; it drove the shaft and was then expelled in a whoosh. That whoosh, which became a fast-repeated foosh-foosh, identified the steam engine; generations of children have played trains hissing foosh-foosh and shuffling forward.

In an internal combustion engine, a mixture of the fuel and air explodes when it is compressed and an electric spark ignites it. So electricity had to come before the engine could be invented. But not all fuels explode that way. As the fuel explodes, it is spent; it has to be quickly removed and new fuel has to be brought into the cylinder for the next explosion. The fuel has to be able to move fast; only fluid fuels can. And not all fluids will explode; only some concentrated fuels—fuels with a high enough octane number—do.

The standard fuel of the nineteenth century was coal—quite the wrong fuel for an internal combustion engine. But when coal is burnt with too little air, it creates carbon monoxide, a highly explosive mixture. If coal is fully burnt with enough air, it creates carbon dioxide, which does not burn at all. If the two gases are judiciously mixed, they can be used to make a hybrid gas which burns with a flame, unlike coal which glows at best. The Europeans found this property useful; they built gasworks to make 'town gas' from coal, and piped it to homes, hotels, theatres and opera houses for lighting. The closed gasworks across the river from the House of Parliament in London dates from those times.

This town gas was the fuel for the first internal combustion engine—one invented by Jean-Joseph Lenoir in 1860. Lenoir fitted one of his engines into a carriage and drove it seven miles in 1863. It took an hour and a half each way—about as fast as a man could walk. He even sold one of his carriages to Tsar Alexander II of Russia. But a carriage could not have carried much town gas, and a gas-fired engine could not develop enough power to go at any speed, so it proved a non-starter.

But just about this time, mineral oils were becoming more generally available as fuels. Crude oil was to be found on or close to the ground in the United States and Russia, and when underground, was under such pressure that a hole punched to it led to a fountain—a gusher. Soon it was discovered in other areas, and began to be mined. Its main use was as an illuminant to replace town gas. But only a part of it—paraffin or kerosene—was a satisfactory lighting fuel. Heavier parts were like liquid coal—they were good for heating but not for lighting. And lighter parts burnt off too rapidly, if they did not explode. These different parts evaporated at different temperatures. So techniques were soon developed to boil the crude oil without air, and to siphon off different distillates as they evaporated.

Of them, the light distillate—petrol, gasoline or motor spirit—was ideal for an internal combustion engine; in 1873, Nicholas-August Otto patented a four-stroke engine which was the precursor of today's vehicle engines. He was not interested in powering vehicles, but his employee, Gottlieb Daimler, was. Daimler started his own workshop, and in 1885, installed an engine on a bicycle. The problem was that it takes much more power to get a vehicle moving than to keep it moving, and the engines of that time were not powerful enough. Daimler tried to get around the problem of weight by using a bicycle, which had two side-wheels like today's kids' bicycles.

At the same time, Karl Benz in Mannheim made a tricycle powered with an internal combustion engine: a four-wheeled vehicle was not a good idea at that time because of difficulties of steering. A horse carriage could be steered by turning the horse's face left or right; but a horseless carriage did not understand such directions. The only way was to turn the front axle on a pivot; that could be very dangerous in a vehicle which could not be easily slowed down.

Benz ran his car around Mannheim mostly at night to keep out of the way of the police. But one day, his wife Bertha wanted to visit her relatives in Pforzheim, some fifty miles away.

> . . . she was egged on by her fifteen-year-old son Eugen to take the car rather than travelling conventionally by train. Together with her younger son Richard, they set out early one morning, leaving a note for Karl to say that they were not deserting him. They made good progress as far as Heidelberg but, on the steeper hills of the Black Forest, Bertha and Eugen had to dismount, leaving thirteen-year-old Richard at the tiller.
>
> On downhill stretches, the leather brake linings wore out, and fresh leather had to be obtained from cobblers. The resourceful Bertha lent a hatpin to clear a blocked fuel pipe, and when an ignition wire short-circuited she took off her garter to insulate the wire.

> Throughout their journey, they were a source of amazement, and in a Black Forest inn a fight nearly broke out between two peasants disputing as to whether the car was driven by clockwork or by a supernatural agency. Nevertheless, Pforzheim was reached before nightfall, and the family made a safe return journey five days later.
>
> (G.N. Georgano, *Cars 1886-1930*, Nordbok, Gothenburg, 1985, p.16.)

That is how the first car was launched; in the following years, Benz made a number of replicas and sold them.

But even then, the motor vehicle did not succeed immediately as a personal vehicle. The big market at that time was for mass transport; the 1880s and 1890s were the heyday of the tram. So the internal combustion engine was applied first to buses, which could accommodate a large enough engine to power the bulk to be moved. The car was for the rich; it imitated and replaced their horse carriages. Like horse carriages, the early models of cars were called Victorias if they had a hood and Phaetons if they did not. Station wagons were so called because they were used to transport luggage and servants from and to the railway station. As late as in 1921, there was one car for every 180 Britons, 200 Frenchmen and 1000 Italians. Only the US had a car for every twenty-seven Americans, because of the revolution brought about by Ford's Model T.

By the time India started urbanizing, buses had overtaken trams in cheapness and speed; the few tram lines that had been built in Indian cities were dismantled and replaced by buses, except in Calcutta. But everywhere in India, buses were taken over by the government in the 1950s. Public ownership meant two things: classless travel, and constant political pressure to keep fares low. Low fares meant losses for the bus companies, and no one would invest in the loss-making companies, so the services became increasingly inadequate. Thus low fares went with overcrowding, and unreliable service. Some city bus services have coped better than others; some have tried partial privatization by leasing in buses. But generally, the services are cheap and of low quality; anyone who can afford it tries to avoid them. This is what has fuelled the demand for personal vehicles in India (see table 3).

And those who want to get on to their own vehicles have been helped by the passage of time. Internal combustion engines have been miniaturized, and can power anything as small as a kid's bicycle. The miniaturization led to the invention of the scooter, soon after World War II, in which a small engine, tucked away under the seat, is enough to carry a portly, sedentary gentleman and his family. Cars have been built in millions, and have turned into standardized commodities at the cheaper end; the Volkswagen Beetle, the Morris Minor and the Citroën Deux Chevaux were produced virtually unchanged for decades. Standardization brought cars within the reach of people of modest means. In our country, this plebianization of the car did not happen because the government decided that the car was not for the people; but something like that is happening just now to two-wheelers.

Over a half of the households in India had a bicycle in 1995-96; apart from watches, there was no consumer durable with more widespread ownership. But the bicycle is a poor man's vehicle; it calls for much exertion, and hence it cannot be used for long distances. It is actually inferior to a bus; in cities where bus services have expanded, the use of bicycles has declined. Hence anyone who can afford it graduates to a scooter, motor cycle or moped. Their ownership intensity tripled in the decade up to

1995-96; by then, probably a tenth of the households had a motorized two-wheeler. The rich probably had more two-wheelers than bicycles; in every income group, two-wheelers were being bought in preference to bicycles. We do not have similar figures for cars, which were owned by some 1.5 per cent of the households in 1995-96; but those who could afford it were similarly changing over from two-wheelers to cars.

This rising ownership of personal vehicles causes worry. Is it not responsible for rising atmospheric pollution? It certainly is; but the pollution they cause can be controlled. Many cities in industrial countries had as polluted air in the 1960s as Indian cities now have; London was sooty, and traffic policemen in Tokyo had to wear masks. But pollution limits were imposed in those cities; today, it is possible to walk about in them without any discomfort.

More serious is congestion. The road space taken by a user is equal to the area occupied by his vehicle, divided by the number of passengers it carries. The area should include not only the area of the vehicle, but also the safe distance between it and other vehicles. Reckoned this way, a bicycle or scooter occupies roughly six square metres. A car occupies about four times as much, whilst a forty-seater bus occupies almost twenty times as much.

But that space is occupied only during the time the vehicle is on the road; and the faster it travels, the less long it will be on the road. If we reckon in this factor, a bicycle is actually the most space-intensive vehicle on the road. Suppose cycles travel at 10 kilometres, cars at 50 kilometres and scooters and buses at 25 kilometres an hour. Then cyclists will occupy three times as much time-space as car passengers and 2½ times as much as passengers on scooters or in buses. If you are rich enough to own a bus and prefer to travel alone in it, you would still be occupying only eight times as much road space-time as a cyclist. When environmentalists campaign for the bicycle and against motor vehicles, they are thinking of something other than economizing road use.

TABLE 4
Road use-intensity of vehicles

	Bicycle	Scooter	Car	Bus
Length (m)	2	2	6	21
Breadth (m)	1	1	2.5	4
Area (sq m)	2	2	15	84
Safety margin (sq m)	4	4	10	16
Total area (sq m)	6	6	25	120
Average speed (km/h)	10	25	50	25
Space-time occupied (sq m-h/km)	0.6	0.24	0.5	4.8
Maximum passengers	2	2	5	40
Minimum area per passenger (sq m)	3	3	5	3
Space-time per passenger (sq m-h/km)	0.3	0.12	0.1	0.12

This is a fair comparison if every vehicle is occupied by only one passenger; if it is occupied by more, the space per passenger falls proportionately. If all the vehicles carry their full load (without standing passengers on buses, children in the boots of cars or infants suckling their mothers on the back seats of scooters), the space taken per passenger comes out to be about the same in all vehicles except the car, in which they occupy almost twice as much space.

But the actual space taken by a passenger depends crucially on the number of passengers in a vehicle; if a bus has only one passenger, he will take far more space than a car driver. Hence one way of economizing road space is to make people fill up vehicles. This is what they do in Singapore; if a car driver wants to drive into the city centre during rush hour, he has to have a full carload. If you give a lift to people waiting for a bus to the next town in the Himalayan hills, they will offer you some money. That is a good idea; I wish more motorists needed the money.

But cars and buses can save space only if they can move at speed; they must not be obstructed by slower traffic. So if there is going to be slow-moving traffic, road use can be improved if fast and slow traffic are segregated. This is obvious in the case of pedestrians. City roads have pavements to segregate slow-moving pedestrians from faster moving vehicles.

The problem with such segregation is that the space given to each type of traffic cannot always be in proportion to the traffic; if it is not, there will still be congestion in one lane while another one is underused. If that happens, the vehicles that face congestion will spill over into lanes not meant for them.

We can see this in Chandni Chowk in Delhi; there are so many pedestrians that they spill on to the road and obstruct wheeled traffic. Traffic in Chandni Chowk would move faster if space for it was reduced and pavements for pedestrians were widened.

The same holds true for bus lanes. They work very well in some western cities—for instance, Berlin—cars simply do not enter bus lanes even when the lanes are empty. In India, on the other hand, bus lanes have never worked. Scooters spill into bus lanes, and buses overtake each other and lumber into lanes for other traffic. The solution that would work in India is the pavement solution. Pavements are for the exclusive use of pedestrians, and no vehicle gets on them because they are raised. Similarly, roads should as far as possible be dedicated to similar traffic—there should be roads for cycle rickshaws only, scooters only, four-wheeled traffic only. All vehicles would move faster if they kept to their kind.

That is the command solution to road access. There can also be a solution based on incentives. Access to roads can be taxed; the tax should be based on the space-time intensity of vehicles. And access to more heavily used roads should cost more than access to little-used by-lanes. Thus a pedestrian or a cyclist would pay heavy road access charges for being so slow; and a licence to go to Chandni Chowk in Delhi or Princess Street in Bombay would cost the earth.

Such charges would be quite impracticable unless price controls on hired vehicles—buses, taxis, scooter rickshaws—were removed. Such vehicles would pay heavy annual road user charges whether they go on the roads at all or not. With such high fixed charges, they would probably have to charge passengers a high entry fee. Fares would be extra, and would be based on mileage as now. Fixed fares work well only if the chances of picking up a fare are roughly equal throughout the city. They never are, so invariably, bus services are inadequate in sparsely populated areas, and auto rickshaw drivers bargain for higher fares to go to such areas. Rather than fix fares which it cannot enforce, the government should leave fares to be fixed between the driver and the passenger. Instead, it should set up taxi stands and bus terminals; vehicles using such stands would have to charge standard fares worked out amongst the vehicle owners themselves.

These arrangements are so different from the ones we are used to that they sound unrealistic. They cannot be put into place overnight; but if they are introduced slowly and with enough notice to everyone, they would improve the quality of life in our cities enormously. It would become expensive for offices and shops to locate in congested areas, and they would move out. Moving around would become expensive, and people would move closer to where they work and shop. More day-to-day business would be done within neighbourhoods, and long-distance commuting as is common now would become unfashionable. Roads would be uncongested, and the rich would be able to cycle around cities. For the less affluent, there would be airconditioned minibuses with plush seats and personal videos.

Work savers

When people think of consumer durables, they tend to think of devices that save work. Our conception of life in rich countries is that people there have all kinds of machines which save time and take drudgery out of domestic life—vacuum cleaners, dishwashers and microwave ovens. But they have such wonderful devices not simply because they are rich, but also because their poor are richer than ours. They buy dishwashers because house maids are expensive or difficult to come by—or because even when they are available, they insist on being given mechanical help. Thus a friend of mine in the British countryside has given the key of her house to a village lady. This lady drops by when she gets time, and uses my friend's washing machine to wash clothes, her dishwasher to wash the dishes, her Hoover to clean the carpets. In other words, my friend has to own all the labour-saving machines because she would not be able to get any house help if she did not have them. When the maid comes, she is treated like royalty: she is served tea and chatted up most cordially. Such are the privileges of living in a rich society.

Those privileges are not for our society; our poor would not impose such labour-saving standards, let alone get such respect. So it is no wonder that table 3 is rather sparse on work-saving machines. Washing machines are just beginning to make inroads into Indian drudgery; 3 per cent of the households had them in 1995-96. What is interesting is that over a third of the rich families had them; clearly they prefer the gentle touch of a Bosch to an unfeeling domestic mangling clothes and beating the life out of them.

The other two work savers in the table have a peculiarly Indian flavour. Three-quarters of mixer-grinders were sold in the South and the West, and are obviously related to the food habits—they are used to grind coffee, spices and lentils. They have undergone an interesting evolution. Before the arrival of machines, these foods used to be milled by hand between heavy rollers. The first mechanical devices were imitations of the manual ones: a motor rotated a heavy roller in a big conical container. These antediluvian monsters can still be seen in the back kitchens of some restaurants in the South. But this Indian innovation has been replaced in the past ten years by an adaptation of the western coffee grinder and food processor. Here is an invention that has truly taken drudgery out of Indian women's lives—in the same way as the streetcorner grain mill did a century ago. Today the grain miller is also on his way out, being replaced by big millers marketing branded flour. The mixer-grinder may also be a transitional phenomenon, to be replaced by branded makes of spices. The process we saw in the comparison of Indian and American consumption, namely the industrialization of food processing, has arrived here too.

The sewing machine has long been popular in northern India. It was long a northern tradition to give a bride a sewing machine as part of her dowry, so that she could sew clothes for her new family in her spare time. Tailors, where available, were useful for men's and ceremonial clothes; women's and children's clothes were made at home by women. Singer machines were imported for generations for this market.

Then in the 1950s, Usha started making sewing machines. By the late 1960s, Usha and Singer sewing machines were being copied by numerous backyard manufacturers in Punjab. Sewing machines became dirt-cheap. They were thus devalued as dowry gifts. At the same time, tailoring became accessible to many more people. That was the beginning of the readymade garment industry. Today, children's clothes are routinely bought readymade even in rural areas; men's garments are increasingly bought readymade. Like food processing, garment making is also getting industrialized.

Conveniences

The British Parliament is housed in the palace of Westminster; it has a tower which could be seen for miles before the advent of high-rise buildings. The reason was that industry and commerce brought regular hours of work for many people who could not afford a watch (those were the days of a foppish pocket watch which was dangled on a gold chain). So they had to look up a clock; clock towers were a central feature of neighbourhoods. With the British they came to India too; there is a clock on the Rajabai Tower of Bombay University, Chandni Chowk had one, and the clock is the most prominent feature of Calcutta's India Exchange Place. And clocks by themselves were not enough; they had loud chimes so that they could be heard from afar.

This world of people having to keep time without having the means to know time has passed very recently in

India. Even as late as the 1970s, wristwatches were the mark of the middle class; the poor asked what the time was. Alarm clocks were more common, but still not widespread. Then came the quartz revolution; quartz clock movements became very cheap, and with them, watches. First they were smuggled in; it was easy to carry a couple of hundred watches in a briefcase. Then, in the early 1990s, import of clock movements was opened up, and the output of cheap watches shot up. That is the story told by table 3; the proportion of households owning mechanical watches rose from 46 per cent in 1985-86 to 82 per cent in 1995-96, but the proportion of families owning quartz watches rose from 9 to 38 per cent. In 1995-96, 37 per cent of the buyers of mechanical watches were farmers; 20 per cent were wage earners. For quartz watches, 25 per cent were farmers and 12 per cent were wage earners.

Pressure cookers were the next most important convenience goods; a quarter of the households had them in 1995-96. Pressure cookers save time as well as energy. They are a niche product: they are useful for boiling; rotis, an indispensable part of north Indian cuisine, cannot be made on them. They are for small families that eat together; in extended families where members keep dropping in for food, they are not so useful. And they need an intense fire, such as from gas or kerosene; a dung-burning chulah would not go with a pressure cooker.

It is surprising that geysers have found such limited use; a hot bath is a worthwhile luxury at all times except in summer. It appears that even amongst the well-to-do, many make do with water heated on a stove or bathe in cold water. The use of geysers has much to do with the climate; for instance, more storage geysers are sold in northern India with its severe winters, whilst instant heaters are more often sold in the South or the West.

An iron is the most useless convenience that can be thought of. Instead of saving work, it actually creates work; its result lasts from a few days to a few hours, after which it has to be repeated. The product—a charcoal iron—and the process—mindless drudgery—suggest that the iron must have an ancient origin; its futility would suggest that it was bound to be made redundant by innovation. First there were knitted garments; initially concealed as underwear, they have progressively moved out as casual wear and become ever more showy. Then there were non-iron garments, which could actually be ironed and held crease well; these have been the rage in India, and the share of the synthetics that are used to make them in total fibre consumption has gone up steadily. But there is a third stage of clothes which cannot hold crease however long they are ironed. Such eternally baggy clothes are still confined to arty people in most countries, but have become common wear in Japan and Germany. The death of the iron cannot be far.

Comforters

Finally, we come to two of the most important sets of goods which make life more tolerable or enjoyable—entertainment systems and cooling systems.

Entertainment is age-old; but it was originally a service. Artists performed before audiences; each performance served only its audience. Thus monarchs had their own entertainers—troubadours, jesters, dancers, fighting animals. The Greeks democratized entertainment; they built amphitheatres for performance of plays. The Romans magnified them into colossea, and used them for gladiatorial fights. These huge open-air theatres would have been quite inappropriate for the cold and wet parts of Europe further north; there emerged indoor entertainments such as opera, ballet and concerts.

The reach of these entertainments was limited, and the cost enormous. Theatres were major investments which often took years to build. Performers often cost little; sometimes, as in the case of contests amongst prisoners or captive animals, they cost no more than upkeep. Still, live entertainment was a privilege. What the modern inventions—sound and picture reproduction systems—have done is to make a performance infinitely reproducible at negligible cost, and to make it distributable across enormous distances.

Radios were the prime source of domestic entertainment sixty years ago. They were expensive; not many people had them. And they were huge—as big as a 29-inch television. The microwave signal they received through an aerial was converted into sound by the vibration of a mica strip. India was almost the monopoly producer of mica.

Radios were also very useful for communication in the armed forces during a war. During World War II, the Allies got seriously worried that India would fall into Japanese hands and mica supplies would stop. Hence there was frantic search for a substitute, and the semiconductor was invented. It eventually led to a lot of things, including computers, but immediately it could be used to make more compact, light and reliable radios. Around the turn of the century, when India was the monopoly supplier of indigo, the Germans invented azo dyes and destroyed the market for indigo within a few years. Fifty years later, the market for mica also underwent a similar contraction with the coming of the semiconductor.

At that time our National Physical Laboratory had a

scientist called Ramamurti who watched the decline of mica with anguish. He had a brainwave: make a simple mica-based radio which could be produced cheaply; it would be sold in millions, revive the demand for mica, and could be used to educate and entertain the whole of India. He tried diligently to get the government to fund his ambitious project, but it never materialized. Instead, the transistor cheapened the radio so much that by 1995-96, 43 per cent of families in India had a radio.

The interesting thing is that radio ownership reaches 53 per cent amongst the not-so-poor; after that it hardly rises as incomes increase. Those who can afford it no longer buy a radio; they buy a television set. Television is the prime entertainer of our time.

Radio is not the only medium that television has replaced; across the world, it has led to the contraction of the public cinema. Only thirty years ago, cinema was the prized entertainment of the middle class; going to an airconditioned cinema hall was a luxury, with which were combined an ice cream in the interval and a dinner in a restaurant afterwards. Students boasted about which latest films they had seen, and developed crushes on actors and actresses. Cinema brought romance into middle-class lives.

As television invaded homes, these social ceremonies ceased, and families huddled together in drawing rooms. Cinema halls filled with those who could not afford a television set. As television ownership broadened, cinema halls emptied. Vast cinema halls were replaced by small neighbourhood theatres showing films of interest to small audiences.

Now a further change is coming. With the arrival of digital broadcasts, a television will offer much more choice. The results can be seen in the United States, where television station licensing is more liberal and the number of stations is consequently larger; channels have specialized in news, films, geographical wonders, music, high-brow entertainment and so on. With the multiplication of channels, television will begin to offer audiovisual experiences which are not thought of as entertainment yet, such as educational courses, do-it-yourself knowhow, medical advice and browsing as on the internet.

Thus, television has increased the variety of experiences available within the home, and reduced the volume of social entertainment available. But a new type of social entertainment has arisen to take the place of theatre, opera and cinema—the shopping mall. Shopping malls are cafeterias of social experience—of activities undertaken together with crowds. In this way, the structure of entertainment is being transformed in the richer countries; the change will come to India as well, in a few years from now.

Cinema halls would have been impossible without air conditioning; before its advent, closed halls existed only in cold northern countries, and they were heated. Heating enclosed spaces is much easier than cooling it: all you do is to light a fire somewhere, and conduct heat from it to where you are sitting. Even then, heating was expensive. Hence the tradition in the cold countries of heating the living room with a fire, whilst the bedrooms were left cold. Now, as people have got rich, they have begun to heat entire houses—generally with electric heaters concealed below the floor or in the walls. But as heat has spread across buildings, the technology of keeping it indoors has also improved; modern buildings are much better insulated than before. Windows are made of metal and fit so well as to be air-tight. They have two panes of glass with space between them from which air is often taken out; the less air there is, the less heat is conducted. Bricks and cement are themselves an insulator; they are poor conductors of heat, which is why they are used for building. But nowadays, the walls themselves are left hollow, and between them, an even better insulator like polyurethane foam is built in. As heating has improved and the consumption of energy for heating has improved, many industrial countries have laid down standards of insulation that new buildings must meet.

There is no easy way of cooling as there is for heating. Before the invention of electricity and the compressor, the only methods of cooling available were passive methods. Thus, old palaces used water courses and fountains to cool the air, the British used verandas, high ceilings and skylights to cut down heat radiation and circulate air, and sadhus used caves in rocks for insulation and for trapping cool air.

All these artifices required either accidental features like natural caves and waterfalls, or specially built structures; and most people in India simply did not have the resources to build such structures. So they did not try to keep cool.

Thus today, the most widespread cooling technology in India is fans; fans are the first device people install after lights when they get electricity. Probably about half the households today have at least one fan. But fans do not cool; they only circulate air. That makes you feel cool by evaporating sweat faster; but it is not very useful if the air is too hot or too humid. Real cooling is possible with air conditioning. Air conditioning is becoming more popular in our country, but we are still at its beginning; it has not become common enough to figure in table 3.

But it will, and it will spread in the same way as heating did in cold countries. The first spaces to get central heating were palaces; the first spaces to get air conditioners were their modern equivalents, the offices of industrial monarchs. Now air conditioning is spreading downwards. If bedrooms were the last to get heated in northern houses, they are the first to get air conditioned in our houses; one can get a good night's sleep under a quilt in a cold bedroom, which is what an air conditioned bedroom makes possible in a hot country. The next spaces that are getting rapidly air conditioned are cars; it is in the merciless midday heat that air conditioning makes the most difference.

But as India gets richer, air conditioning will spread to entire homes, and will make enormous demands on power generation. Already there are restrictions in many cities on the use of air conditioning at peak times. But that is characteristic of a poorly run country, not a poor one. We should be thinking of making air conditioning more energy-efficient—by insulating our houses and cars, by combining air conditioning with water-cooling, and by using modern electronic controls to match the cooling output with needs.

SERVICES

Services are products that have to be used in the very moment they are produced. Whilst people in the US would consume more of most things, one would expect this to be less true of services for two reasons. First, for a service to be provided there has to be a service provider standing by whenever a customer may turn up. The tedium of this waiting around is known only to someone who has minded a shop on a summer afternoon; one has to stand around for customers who never come. American kids serve as shop assistants in summer holidays; they find it hard to accept that they are not allowed to bring their Walkmans to work.

But even without Walkmans, services require humans; they waste much time doing nothing, and even when they are working flat out, their productivity is low. Hence, services will cost more in a richer country where people are paid more, and will be consumed less. And second, we saw that one way people adjust themselves to poverty is by buying things in a less finished form and preparing them for use themselves or through hired help. An obvious example is clothing; as table 2 shows, people in India buy more cloth and fewer garments. If so, they will also be getting the cloth tailored. This is why there would be more demand for services.

We see both these processes at work in table 2. With the exception of food, Indian consumption of major groups of consumer goods—beverages, tobacco products, clothing, footwear, furniture—was less than 6 per cent of the American level. The ratio is much higher for most services. The price differences are also much larger—in general, services are even cheaper in India than in the US.

Thus domestic service costs only 3 per cent in India of what it costs in the US, and household services—those of plumbers, electricians etc—cost 14 per cent as much. And Indian consumption of both is substantial. It may seem surprising that with such cheap domestic service, Indians do not consume more of it than Americans. But as people get richer, they would also use more of their income to pass on tedious and unpleasant chores, and the Americans do this in spite of the fact that domestic service costs so much more.

It is not surprising that Indians travel so much more by bus and rail than Americans—although neither is cheap in India compared to other services. Vehicle ownership is much lower in India, and this is reflected in the demand for hired transport. But even then, Americans use four times as much hired transport. They travel more by air; but apart from that, they hire cars or taxis more often. It is normal for businessmen visiting places to hire a car at the airport and return it when they go back. In some cities, parking is becoming so difficult that people prefer to hire a car when they need one—for instance, to go to a wedding or for a weekend in the countryside. Much of central Paris was built in the nineteenth and early twentieth centuries; the buildings, although they are stately and imposing, were not built to accommodate cars, and most of the parking is on the streets. People are getting so fed up of having to look for a parking space that they are increasingly relying on taxis or hired cars. Some have also started car-owners' cooperatives: they own cars collectively, and hire them out to members by the hour. The earnings are shared amongst the owners. In this way, owners who do not use their cars much actually earn from their fractional car-ownership.

Health and education

The cost of hospitals and doctors in India was surprisingly low in 1973. Even if a doctor were maintained in the state of luxury in India, he would cost only a third as much as in the States. But doctors are far cheaper than that—their services cost less than 2 per cent of what they do in the US. This is not an index of their standard of living, for Indian doctors do probably work harder, or at least longer hours, than American doctors. But even after allowing for differences in productivity, Indian medical services are extremely cheap. Why is this so?

The explanation lies partly in the fact that in 1973, most Indian hospitals were owned by, and doctors employed by, the government. The government follows its own principles of pricing. Wages in the entire government are fixed centrally; doctors' salaries are related to those of a Section Officer or Under Secretary, and are consequently extremely low. Doctors' services are often free; patients pay only for medicines and tests. The low cost leads to relatively high consumption of medical services.

But the cheap medical services also reflect another phenomenon: that teaching and training are cheap in India. In 1973 this was due to the fact that most of the educational system was either owned or controlled by the government; the salaries were fixed by the government, and so were the fees. Since then, much private education has come up, especially in computer services; and education in government-controlled schools and colleges has been backed up by numerous private training schools. The cost of these private services is higher, but not all that high—compared to the United States, it is still extremely low.

What it amounts to is that just as a lump of Indian iron ore can be smelted, treated and shaped into a ball-bearing that compares with one produced in America, so can an Indian child be reared, taught and moulded into a doctor comparable to an American one. Our best teaching institutions do precisely this; over three-quarters of the graduates of the Indian Institutes of Technology emigrate, mostly to the United States. There was a time in the 1960s and 1970s when Britain was prepared to take Indian doctors and young medical graduates were migrating there in thousands.

But if colleges turn out more graduates than can find berths abroad, those graduates will have to find jobs in this country, and their wages will settle down at a much lower level than abroad; their services will be cheap, and the consumption of those services can also be much higher than our standard of living would warrant. That is what we see amongst doctors.

But suppose that those services can reach standards prevalent or required abroad. In that case, one or both of the phenomena we have seen above will occur: the servants will emigrate, or they will export their services. Services have to be consumed wherever and whenever they are produced; but there are ways of selling them abroad. In the case of software services, either engineers go abroad for short periods to provide them—in what is called bodyshopping—or they can embody their services in forms which can be sent over telephone or satellite, be it computer programmes, figures or words. In the case of medical services or hospitality, patients or tourists can come to India, be treated or entertained and sent back.

It is better for a country to export services than to export servants. If servants stay at home, they will provide services to their fellow-countrymen as well. And the money they earn from exports will create income and employment within the country. But just the fact that servants are cheap does not lead to the export of their services. For that the services have to be of the standard, as well as in the form required by foreigners. The services of a doctor sitting in India are not exportable, but if the doctor can offer heart bypass operations in a hospital which offers as good a chance of success as an American hospital at a lower cost, then patients can be attracted from America. There are thousands of hotels in India, but that is not enough to attract foreign tourists; the hotels have to be safe, clean, and they have to offer food the tourists can eat.

Thus export of services needs its own infrastructure and local linkages. But they are not so nearly elaborate as those of traditional industry like metals, chemicals or medicines. Many countries that are too small or misplaced to set up such industries have thrived on services. Thus in Ireland a tax-free zone was set up some twenty years ago to attract financial intermediaries. It was just a set of office buildings with state-of-the-art communication facilities. Today it is one of the world's foremost tax havens, comparable to Luxemberg, Jersey or Bermuda. Honolulu has a beach stretching a couple of miles and hotels on it occupying some eighty acres; they process over 3 million tourists a year.

Government services

If we go by the number of government employees, India is quite well governed: every citizen was served by one-fifth as many employees as in America. But the commodities used by the government to provide its services were only 3 per cent of what the US government used per citizen. In other words, the Indian government employed a lot of people, but the resources they used per employee were only one-seventh of those an average American bureaucrat used.

This poverty of resources shows in simple ways. It is quite exceptional for the Indian government to reply to the letters that it receives; it is the rule in the US. Many government departments give out free brochures about the services they provide or the laws they enforce; that is very unusual in India. All US government departments give telephone numbers on which citizens can get information; it is virtually unknown for departments in India to give information over the phone. The presence of the police on the roads is more evident in the US; in India, one does not often encounter a policeman who is not on traffic duty. American policemen will generally have a car; the Indian policeman is unlikely to have even a bicycle. You walk into government offices in India and cannot escape the impression of inadequate resources.

Suppose your car broke down and you called a mechanic and he came without tools; you would think he was a pretty incompetent mechanic. Why then does the government employ almost 4 million people and give them so little to do their jobs with? It could be because you pay the mechanic for the job done after he has repaired your car, whereas you do not pay the government for catching the thief who picked your pocket or resurfacing the road before your house. It does these things free, and pays the costs out of taxes it takes from you without asking your leave.

Should the government behave like that? Should anyone provide services without charging for them, or impose charges without relating them to services? The answer is yes. If everyone has to pay to catch thieves and murderers, many will never be caught because their victims are not rich enough to have them caught; and criminals may form gangs to raise the cost of catching them even further. It is better to have only one agency to catch and punish miscreants, to give it monopoly of violence, and to charge it with preventing rather than detecting crime; and if such an agency protects all citizens, then it must be financed by subscriptions from them all. Similarly, a road benefits all those who use it; far too few roads will be built if everyone has to contribute to building roads that he needs. A government in principle is useful—indeed, indispensable—where a large number of people live together.

But a government in reality can take many shapes, depending on those who run it and control it. Here I am beginning to run far beyond standards of living, which are the subject of this chapter, and would like to leave standards of governance till the last chapter.

III

Throes of Creation

Goods and services can be pooled into baskets. The standard of living is the basket of goods and services that a person consumes; the cost of living is the cost of the basket. The basket cannot be measured in maunds, inches or litres; nor can the price. But their variations across time and space can be compared; it is possible to say whether it costs more to live in Pune or in Bangalore, or who lives better, single mothers or unwed fathers.

Someone must produce the goods and services that the citizens of a country consume. Some things that are produced may have been exported; they may have paid for imports that were consumed but not produced in the country. If imports exceed exports, a country may be able to consume more than it produces. But for this one exception, a country's production puts a cap on its standard of living. Its citizens can receive gifts from abroad or borrow abroad, and thus live better than their own production would allow. But excepting such windfalls, no country can live better than its output would allow; and its average citizen can live no better than his or her average productivity. Some citizens may be able to live beyond their means if they borrow, receive charity, or live on their savings. But if they consume more than they produce, someone else must produce more than he consumes.

India in particular has no godfather; the aid it receives from abroad is negligible, and all the investment it receives from abroad has to be paid for in interest, dividends and profits. We are poor because we produce little; the only way we can live better is by producing more per person.

What is this production? The idea of production comes weighted with heavy historical associations. The most ancient languages have a word for production; but most things that are being produced today—bicycles, plastic buckets, balloons, aspirin—were not being produced in ancient times.

At the beginning production meant something like birth—like a cow producing a calf. The people of those times had a fertile imagination; it can be seen at work in our heritage of stories, myths and religions. So from cows they went on to Mother Earth, and thought of natural products as production. But they could not really imagine a carpenter 'producing' a chair. Nowadays, when agriculture has become just one of many industries, we do not think of production in strictly biological terms. But we would still like to make a distinction between 'productive' and 'unproductive' activities—'productive' meaning useful, and 'unproductive' meaning useless or harmful. However much such a definition may appeal to us, it would be impossible to agree on one; productive activities would be different for a smoker and a non-smoker, a drinker and a teetotaller, a celibate and a nymphomaniac, or a vegetarian and a meat-eater.

To avoid such sectarian quarrels, it is best to regard everything that can be consumed as having been produced. But more things are produced than are consumed. No one consumes cotton, for instance, but it goes into clothes which are worn; so cotton too must be regarded as produced. So must everything that helps to produce things for consumption—machines, transport services, telephone calls, almost everything we can think of.

So is there anything that is not produced? Is anybody being unproductive? Does a tree produce leaves? Does a chewer of gum produce bubbles? Does a book produce sleep? We must stop somewhere; we must put our foot down and say that production stops here.

If you went and paid for something to consume, it was produced for you. It does not matter who you are. Even if you are a foreigner and the thing was exported to you, it was still produced in India. And if you consumed something that was imported, it was not produced in India. Production is consumption plus exports minus imports.

But suppose something was produced for someone to consume but has not been sold yet; surely it must be regarded as produced. Production must be measured over some period—a day, a month, a year. If something was produced in the year but was not consumed till later, it is part of this year's production. Something that was produced last year and consumed this year is part of last year's production, not this year's.

So production can be measured in the following way: add the value of what is consumed, exported, or added to stocks, and subtract from it what is imported, or used up out of past stocks. No piece of economics is respectable unless it has at least one equation, so let me copy the Keynesian identity from any first-year textbook:

$$Yt = Ct + (Kt - K[t - 1]) + (Xt - Mt)$$

where Y is the value of production, C is the value of consumption, K is the stock of goods at the end of a period (all goods, whether they are meant for consumption or not), X is exports, M is imports, the subscript t stands for a period, and t – 1 for the previous period;

(Kt – K[t – 1]) thus stands for the change in stocks over the period t. This definition of national income includes only some goods and services that are produced—only those that are either consumed, carried over from one period to the next, or exported in excess of imports. These are called final goods.

But production is not organized for the convenience of economists; many people produce something, not for consumption, but to sell to other producers—bricks for builders, sleepers for railways, buttons for tailors. These are all intermediate goods (for brevity, let us include services). Where does their production figure? They cannot enter the equation above; but it can be shown that they are all hidden in it. For any final good will have been produced in some outfit—let us call it a firm. The firm will have purchased various intermediate goods, and then worked on them to produce the final good. Similarly, those intermediate goods will have been produced by some other firm; it too will have bought intermediate goods and worked on them to make what it sells. At each stage, firms add value to the intermediate goods they buy; this value added is the difference between the value of goods they sell and the goods they buy.

Thus the value of every final good—the value at which it was bought—can be decomposed into the sum of value added in its production, plus the value added in the production of the intermediate goods that went into it. For the economy, the sum of expenditures on final goods is equal to the sum of value added in the production of all goods. (Well, almost; if the government levies taxes on goods, the value of purchases of those goods will exceed the value of their sales, and hence the total value added, by the amount of the tax revenue.) It can hence be expressed as the sum of value added in each industry.

What happens to all that value added? It is what remains after purchases from outsiders are paid for; hence it is what those who own or work in the firm get. It is the sum of incomes generated by the firm. For the country, therefore, it can be expressed as the sum of incomes—wages, salaries, profits, dividends, interest, rents earned by the citizens of the country. Hence it is called national income. But it is also equal to national expenditure on final goods—or national product—that is, the sum of value added in different productive activities.

Finally, a squiggle regarding the change in stocks which figures in the equation above of national expenditure. It includes, for instance, machinery which survives from one year to the next; the change in the stocks of machinery is the value of machinery at the end of the year minus its value at the beginning of the year. But some of the machinery which came in at the beginning will have been scrapped; the rest will have become older and less valuable. How much less? No one can tell. For old machinery is not being bought and sold, so we cannot use its market value. It lasts for many years. As it gets older, it begins to break down, and needs more maintenance. Finally it breaks down completely. Often it is scrapped before it does so. It is impossible to place a precise value on the wear-and-tear, or depreciation, of machinery. We can put some approximate value on it and subtract it from the value of machinery at the end of the period; in that case we get the national product net of depreciation, or net national product for short. If we ignore depreciation and just take the gross additions to the stock of machinery during the year, we get gross national product.

This national product consists of what is produced within the country, as well as income received from abroad—income on investments, earnings of Indians abroad, charity received from abroad, etc. If we take this income out of national product, we get domestic product. This is how we come to the four magnitudes we keep running into in economic discussions: gross and net national product, and gross and net domestic product.

With this rather arcane introduction, we can begin to ask the question: what determines production? How does a counry get richer or poorer?

INGREDIENTS

The simplest way is to ask what goes into production. One classification that was produced in the early days of economics conceived that everything was produced by three primary factors of production: land, capital and labour. Land was all resources—earth, trees, minerals, etc.—which was not produced by human labour. Capital was all durable resources produced with human labour. Labour was all human effort, manual or mental. All other inputs were produced by varying combinations of these three.

This classification still continues in textbooks, but finds little use in economics as it is practised. Economic theories often assume an unspecified number of factors of production with little to distinguish between them. We have no interest in advancing economic theory, only in making the realm of production more comprehensible. So let me make up an arbitrary but more useful distinction between materials, energy, information, labour and finance.

Materials

We generally think of materials as solid though, of course, liquid and gaseous materials also enter production processes. Nitrogenous fertilizers, for instance, can be produced out of air and water. The world's first nitrogenous fertilizer was animal manure, which is still used on a large scale. Then, in the mid-nineteenth century, an island was discovered on the west coast of Latin America which was covered with layer upon layer of bird shit. This guano became the favoured fertilizer of Europe. During World War II, however, Europe under German domination could no longer import guano. Germany occupied Norway, which is extremely mountainous and has huge hydroelectric resources. Norsk Hydro, its electricity company, worked out a way of separating nitrogen from air and hydrogen from water by means of electrolysis, combined them to make ammonia, and embodied this ammonia into nitrogenous fertilizer. After the War, water was replaced by mineral oil, chiefly a combination of hydrogen and carbon, which is why petroleum products are called hydrocarbons; today most nitrogenous fertilizer is made from natural gas or lighter products of mineral oil akin to petrol. The modern chemical industry prefers to work with gases or liquids, which are easier to mix together and move around than solids.

Still, thinking of solid materials helps to visualize the change that has come in the realm of production. Solid materials last, and leave a record. Three types of materials—materials for construction, for tools, and for clothing—illustrate the history of technology.

The commonest material of human use is silicon, the chief ingredient of building materials as well as earthen vessels. It is so central that ancient civilizations are described by the vessels they left behind. Thus the north Indian civilization of the second millennium BC is known as the Painted Grey Ware civilization. An ancient Greek artefact can be readily recognized by the reddish designs on orange vessels. Ming pottery has to have blue dragons on a white background. Maybe when the present civilizations are buried and rediscovered a few thousand years later, advanced people with pointed ears will examine Noritake pottery and Wedgwood figurines and admire our cleverness.

They will also note the great change that came in construction materials over the past two centuries, and which is still going on in India—the change from straw, wattle and wood to brick and, more lately, to steel, concrete and glass. Straw is an excellent insulator, but it is not surprising that it is going out of fashion. It is laborious to work with, and does not last long; it has to be replaced every three to four years. In England they still preserve some thatched cottages. Only a few people still know how to make them or replace them; they are paid extremely well. They make thatches eight to twelve inches thick to make them impermeable to water and to the biting winter winds; bathe them in preservatives to make them last longer; and wrap them in wire mesh to make sure the roofs do not blow off or come unstuck. Although the modern thatch is more durable and weatherproof, it is so costly that only a few well-heeled Englishmen have thatched cottages. Straw dwellings are much cheaper in India. Still, everyone who has the choice prefers a pucca house; in fact, the proportion of population living in pucca houses is a good index of prosperity.

So why do people continue to live in huts of straw? It is because bricks need heat to make, and that heating energy is still too expensive for many Indians.

The story of better housing is a story of more affordable energy. Energy becomes more affordable both as people's incomes rise and as the cost of energy in terms of other goods falls. Bricks are heavy, and their cost rises rapidly with distance. Clay that can be used to make bricks is widespread, so brick kilns are spread all over. But every brick kiln needs fuel. As population has grown, firewood has become increasingly scarce. And mineral coal is cheap only near the mines in Bihar and Bengal; the further away one goes, the more expensive it is. Still, as people's incomes have gone up relatively to the cost of brick and mortar, they have progressively replaced straw huts with pucca houses.

Cement needs limestone, which is less widely distributed than brick clay. So cement factories are fewer and far between. They also use coal. As incomes have gone up, the use of cement has also gone up.

Cement houses are much stronger than brick houses, especially if a skeleton of steel is wrapped with cement—reinforced. So cement is generally used for floors and ceilings, and can support larger buildings, such as apartment and multistorey buildings. Even in such buildings, however, cement is used for bearing the load in columns and beams, and cheaper bricks are often used for walls which do not need strength. But the more people live in towns, and the more expensive land becomes, the taller will buildings be, and the greater will be the use of cement.

Next only to building materials are materials used for making tools. The earliest tools were made by chipping hard stones, and later by shaping wood. Even after the art of smelting metals was discovered, they were sparingly used, for their fuel costs were even higher than those of bricks and mortar. Most metallic ores contain compounds of metals, and metals can be separated from them by heating them with materials which combine with and remove the nonmetallic elements in the compounds. Thus, many ores are oxides of metals; the oxygen can be removed by heating the ore with some reducing element which would combine with it—for instance, carbon in charcoal or coal which would take the oxygen to make carbon dioxide.

Metals that melted at lower temperatures were the first to be made. Copper melts at 700°C; copper and its alloys, bronze and brass, were the earliest metals to be used. Iron, which melts at 1600°C, could not be properly melted till the eighteenth century. But various impurities in iron give it very useful properties. For instance, iron contaminated by carbon is steel; it is stronger than pure iron. Iron ore in different places had different impurities, and produced iron with different qualities. Hence crafts made on local iron developed in many places. It was particularly useful for weapons—swords, shields, spears, chainmail etc.; ironmaking industries flourished wherever there was warfare. It was also very useful in nails for joining pieces of wood, for instance in making ships. So the use of iron expanded rapidly.

But its appetite for fuel was enormous. Iron making denuded forests so quickly that it could be produced only in small quantities. Then, in the eighteenth century, Britain ran out of wood to make charcoal, and pioneered the use of mineral coal in iron making. That began the era of iron and steel which still continues. Steel was used to make tools, to reinforce cement and concrete structures, and to make machines. Today it is the most ubiquitous material in use, and comes in hundreds of different compositions—alloys—and thousands of shapes; the world produces about 800 million tons of iron and steel a year.

Aluminium is the commonest metal in the earth's surface; it is present in clays, and forms such beautiful gems as rubies and sapphires. But the composition of bauxite, the form in which aluminium is mostly found, is such that aluminium cannot be separated simply with heat. It was separated only in 1863, and became industrially available in the 1880s. It is light, strong and a good conductor of electricity. But it needs electricity to produce. It is largely produced in countries with very cheap hydroelectricity. As it has got cheaper, it has begun to replace steel in uses where light weight is useful, as in vehicles.

The three metals, copper, iron and aluminium, with their alloys, have made the construction of modern machinery possible; they are thus the foundation of the huge increases in human productivity that have occurred in the past two centuries.

Finally, things that can be wrapped around—for instance, clothes. The earliest humans hunted for food, and wrapped the killed animals' skins around themselves. Skins are particularly good protection against cold. But in heat, animals can bear to wear skins only because water from their blood comes out through the pores of their skins, evaporates and keeps them cool. This cooling system stops once the skin is taken off the animals. So it is better to have porous clothing; air can come in through the pores, and sweat can exit. That is how, once the art of spinning and weaving them was discovered, fibres came to be preferred for clothes. People used the fibres that were locally available. Those who had hairy animals used animal hair such as wool, alpaca and pashmina; those in the delta of the Ganges used jute; those living in dryer areas grew cotton; and the Philipinos used ramie, a rather effete, somewhat see-through kind of fibre. Nowadays, when the President of Philippines is visited by foreign dignitaries, be they the King of Tonga or the Sultan of Brunei, he presents them with an embroidered shirt made of ramie and gets himself photographed with them.

Although everyone attired himself in his or her national fibre, however, India produced cheap and abundant cotton, and with its help, became an exporter of cotton clothes. Since the others had nothing that Indians needed in such quantity, they had to pay in gold, silver and gems. It was these imported treasures that gave India its fame as a rich country—until the British invented mechanical spinning and weaving in the eighteenth century and captured the markets. In the next two hundred years, machine-made textiles were the foundation of industrialization of one country after another—India, Japan, Korea, Hong Kong.

Then in this century, a way was discovered of making fibres by fiddling with the molecules of hydrocarbons; with that, new fibres came to be made out of mineral oil and gas. In the past fifty years, they have become ever cheaper and have taken an increasing share of the clothing market. India, being the home of cotton and of handlooms, tried to keep down synthetic fibres by taxing them. But in the 1990s, even our government has recognized that we Indians would be clothed better and more cheaply if nylon and polyester were cheaper. So finally in 1998, synthetic fibres outstripped cotton as clothing material in India.

The substitution started first and went furthest in the industrial countries. A time came when synthetics came to be looked down upon as cheap, and cotton acquired a new respect for being expensive. New ways of processing cotton were developed. My most treasured pair of trousers is a dark green German one. The airline had lost my bag and given me some money to go and buy clothes. I walked into a vast clothes shop and picked up this pair off the shelf. It is smooth as silk. It is double layered and hence is warmer than any woollen pair.

But it is not only textile fibre that can be made from oil and gas. Polymerization—as this manipulation of molecules is called—can yield almost anything—panels for walls, wool for insulation, mouldings for car dashboards, housings for motors, catgut for suturing after operations, film for movies, lining for canals. Where these were earlier made of other materials, the synthetic substitutes are cheaper and generally of better and more consistent quality. Today, plastic bags and bottles are a nuisance. That is because they have become dirt cheap. There was a time not many decades ago when everyone carried a cloth bag for shopping, and when poor people treasured the one bottle they used to go and buy kerosene in.

Energy

Energy provides both heat and motive power. It is thus essential to all cooking processes—including metal smelting—and all moving machinery. But heat and motive power got married only with the invention of the steam engine by Thomas Newcomen in 1712. Till then, motive power was provided by wind and water. Wind is a weak source. In a few windy places it could drive a windmill; it could also push ships around on certain seas and in certain seasons. Water is even more limited; it flows fast enough to harness only in wet and hilly places. Elsewhere, animals and human beings provided motive power; and as I shall describe in a later section, physiology limits their productivity.

What steam power did was to breach this limit; a steam-driven economy could be far more productive than a labour-driven one. But only in activities to which steam power could be applied. It could drive a piston back and forth; this is why the Newcomen engine was applied to draw water out of coal mines—just as a pump draws water out of a well or a river today. This was enormously useful in Britain, a wet country where coal mines were getting deeper and deeper; but otherwise, there were not many uses.

Then a crank shaft was attached to the piston, and its back-and-forth motion was converted into rotary motion; this opened up many more uses. Water-driven wheels were already driving spinning frames and flour mills in northern England; these were the uses to which steam was first applied.

But the rotary motion could be conveyed only as far as the shaft reached. An entire line of spinning frames could be attached to a single shaft; but the number was limited by the length of the shaft. Hence industry required a lot of steam engines, with their cost and their requirements of coal and water. Steam-based industry was costly: it needed a lot of capital, for the user industry, for the coal industry, and for transporting coal.

Of this, transport of coal was really expensive, because it had to be transported by animals. This is why Britain constructed an extensive network of canals. Along both sides were bridle paths; heavy horses walked along the paths and pulled coal barges. But canals were expensive, and their capacity was limited. One tow-horse could not overtake another; so barges had to follow in a queue crawling along at the speed of the slowest horse.

This is why the steam engine came to be applied to transport. It could carry only a limited quantity of water and coal on which it ran; there had to be coaling and watering stations every few miles. It could run only along rails; the tracks were costly, and required continuous watch and maintenance. Few railways made much profit; but they liberated transport from the constraints placed by animals. Their advantages were so enormous that governments had them built by giving free land and subsidies and armtwisting the many interests involved.

Coal-based industry made labour more productive and countries richer; the riches allowed them to build railways.

But coal and railways were very confining. The story of the nineteenth century is one of concentration. Britain became a world power because of coal. Germany outstripped France as the continental power of Europe because of its rich coal reserves. Eastern United States emerged as an industrial power on the basis of its coal. Within countries, coal confined development. Within Britain, industry was concentrated in coal-rich northern England; within Germany, the Ruhr was the industrial heart. In India, the Bengal-Bihar belt was the most industrialized area right till World War II.

The confining influence of coal was broken by electricity, which arrived in the second half of the nineteenth century. Electricity was much easier and cheaper to deploy: the cable it needed was cheaper than a railway track, the transformers it needed along the way to keep up the voltage cost less to run than coaling stations, and the electric motor which converted it to motive power was less messy and cranky than a steam engine. Initially, electricity was not cheap. Even today, the most efficient power generators convert only 40 per cent of the coal they use into electricity; in the early days, their efficiency was less than 10 per cent. That is why electricity was applied first to lighting and next to traction; it was only in this century that it came to be extensively used for motive power in industry. But once it was so used, it freed industry from the tyranny of the shaft, and allowed factories to become both very big and very small.

Oil did all that coal could, but better. Being liquid, it was easily transported by pipeline and tanker. Forced out of the ground by subterranean pressure, it required no work to mine. Now, old oilfields which no longer yield oil under natural pressure are helped with air, water and steam injection; but even now, a good deal of oil requires no outside energy to mine. Oil has greater energy density: it has roughly 10 kilocalories per gram, whereas coal has about 4—less if it is as mixed up with impurities as Indian coal. Oil could fire a steam engine just like coal; but the three engines developed to use oil—Otto, diesel and turbine—are more compact, and give higher energy efficiency. Since oil emerged in the last years of the nineteenth century to challenge coal, it has never looked back. Our government did its best to halt the march of oil—the foreign fuel—against swadeshi coal. But the cost of doing so was too high, and oil has progressively penetrated India, especially after Bombay High went on stream in the early 1980s.

Oil has made coal and, therewith, electricity much cheaper. Huge diesel-driven excavators have been developed which tear through earth and uncover underground coal; it is no longer necessary for human beings to burrow and tunnel. In an underground coal mine, the height of the shaft limits the size of the machines that can be used. In an open-cast mine, height is no problem; ten-storey-high shovel excavators scoop up and cart coal away.

Oil has become so central to our lives that the spectre of its running out haunts us every once in a while. The fear was at its height when the Arab countries raised the price of oil fourfold in 1973. That attempt to profit from artificial scarcity failed, and for two decades, the price of oil could not even keep up with general inflation. In the past year, the oil producers have raised the price by 50 per cent; if they continue for some time longer, they will again raise a scare of an oil famine.

Thanks to them, however, we now have the experience of one oil crisis. It showed that if necessary, it is possible greatly to increase the efficiency of oil use. Oil is not going to run out suddenly. First the force with which it comes out of the ground will diminish, and more investment and energy will go into secondary recovery—in helping oil come up. Then oil wells will go deeper. Next, oil will have to be obtained from shale, which is solid and has to be mined like coal. So oil will become progressively more expensive. As it does so, more efficient ways of using oil will be invented; and other fuels will be used in its stead. The first substitute will be natural gas, which is already replacing oil in power stations. When gas begins to run out, it will be replaced by coal. All these can be replaced by nuclear energy any time if people and governments work out ways of regulating it.

Thus serious problems of energy shortage are some decades, perhaps centuries away. The important question is not whether fossil fuels will run out, but how fast. That speed can vary enormously, depending essentially on two factors. One is, how far world population grows. If population continues to grow, there will eventually be not just an energy crisis, but a water crisis, a metal crisis, and in general, a constraint on the rise in standards of living. Hence stabilizing population—even reducing it—is the first step to avoiding crises. The other is the eventual living standards and lifestyles. If everyone in the world adopts the American lifestyle, energy will run out much faster than it is doing now. But Japan has already reached a living standard comparable to the American with much lower energy use; it is possible to live well with even lower energy use. Thus changes in population and living style are possible which will postpone, and quite possibly avoid crises.

Intelligence

It is difficult to describe the third input accurately; intelligence is a suitably double-edged word, meaning both thinking ability and information. What I mean is that production processes need to be controlled, and decisions need to be taken to stop them, change their speed, modify them or change them. These decisions are a necessary input into the processes.

This capacity to make decisions is characteristic of human beings; this is why human workers are employed in production. For instance, a spindle does not know when yarn is snapped; it continues to rotate. A human worker sees that the yarn is broken, stops the spinning frame, rejoins the yarn and starts the frame again.

Such decisions can be taken and implemented by non-human devices as well. The simplest example is a safety valve on a steam. When the steam pressure rises so high as to risk an explosion, the safety valve releases steam. A more complicated but still inert device is a governor; if the speed of an engine threatens to exceed a limit, the governor restrains it.

The capacity of such inanimate decision-makers was limited till the advent of computers. Computers contain programmes; these programmes can embody innumerable statements of the type, 'If this happens, do this.' If one can enumerate all the possible events in a process and specify how to react to them, they can be embodied in a computer programme; the programme can then take over decision-making in that area, and no human intervention is necessary.

The most graphic instance of this is a machining centre. There was a time when individual components of a machine had to be shaped by hand. First, a rough shape was made up out of metal by casting it (that is, melting it and pouring it into a mould) or forging it (that is, hammering it into shape). Then this shape was locked into a lathe across two holders which could rotate it at speed. As it rotated, a worker pressed a shaped tool—say, a chisel—against it. Slivers of metal fell off the shape, and slowly it assumed the final shape. This is how precious stones are cut. It is extremely laborious, and it requires a fine eye; that is why almost half of the world's precious stones are sent to India for cutting.

Now, car plants need to perform this metal-shaping operation on a vast scale. A single car plant may produce two cars every minute. Each car has this hideously complicated metal piece called the cylinder block; it houses extremely accurately shaped holes for pistons to move in, smaller holes into which spark plugs are screwed in, other holes through which the fuel-air mixture enters and the exhausted gases go out, all built into a very hard and durable box.

It is a wonder to watch this cylinder block being made in a machining centre. The machining centre is connected to a computer, just like the personal computer in our homes and offices; the instructions to the machining centre are written into a computer programme. The cylinder block is carried into the machining centre. The machining centre has a number of tools held in a rack. A mechanical arm picks up one tool after another, travels to one precise spot above the cylinder block, and bores down to shape one of its areas. It goes on doing this until the cylinder block is perfectly dimensioned. Then it stops, the cylinder block moves away, and another one enters to be beautified. The machining centre is not very different from a women's hairdresser, only more elegant.

A machining centre is a robot. Before they came on the scene, we used to imagine robots as inanimate humanoids, with two legs, two arms, a bulbous head and antennae sticking out. There are such robots; inventors make them to satisfy the human thirst for the familiar. But robots do not have to come in any particular shape. All they have to have is a programmable brain, electric power, and tools to do the programmed work. The cockpit of a plane is a kind of robot; so is the control room of a refinery.

The Japanese are the pioneers of robot manufacture, and have set up factories run entirely by robots. But robots do not run everything even in Japan. Just as steam engines were expensive in their early days, robots are expensive today. Just as steam engines were initially applied to operations which suited their mode of operations—spinning, weaving, locomotion—robots are being applied to sequential, programmable operations. They are particularly at home in metal smelting, treating and shaping, in the mass production of petrochemicals, and in some assembly operations. But just as electric motors have multiplied in size and shape and taken over ever more functions, so will electronic brains.

Labour

I mentioned that the Newcomen engine married heat and motive power. How did things work before the two got married? Before they did, heat could be produced by burning something, but it could not be employed to do work. All motive power was provided by animals and human beings. Both convert energy they absorb in food into energy of movement and work. In this conversion, most of the energy absorbed is lost as heat. Mammals' bodies cannot convert more than a quarter of the energy into motive power. Of this, a good deal is taken away in unproductive activities; not more than 10 to 15 per cent is available for productive activities, such as producing food, clothes, shelter or serving other human beings. Besides, a certain proportion of a human population—children, old people, the sick—would be incapable of productive work. If people live long—say, up to eighty years—take good care of themselves, have as few children as possible—say, two per couple—and continue to work till they fall dead, then perhaps a half of the population might be working. If they die at thirty-five and have eight children as they used to do in ancient times, not more than a quarter might be productive. This means that if a human community is to survive, every productive member of it must produce about fifteen times the food she consumes; if she is fecund or has a husband who keeps going off to war, she would have to produce much more.

Where human beings could not produce fifteen times as much as they consumed, the land was not populated. Elsewhere they could produce enough by hunting and collecting roots and vegetables. But animals and edible plant materials have a natural rate of regeneration; if humans collected more than was being naturally produced, the output of edibles fell, and the humans starved. So hunting and gathering populations were extremely sparse. The subsistence limit kept the population low.

People's diets also adapted to what the land could produce. For instance, dry areas yielded little grain from cultivation, but could support animals that could wander around and eat grass and leaves; in such areas, people ate more meat. In wet areas which grew more vegetation, people ate more roots and vegetables. In the sunny river valleys which were well watered, grain crops grew well, so people ate more grain. These variations in diet, which were originally based on the local natural resources, persist in modern populations even when they are not exclusively dependent on locally produced food.

There were regions where the productivity of food producers exceeded the minimum; they supported denser populations, and more of their people did something other than food production. India and China, for instance, were the most populous countries of the world because an average worker in those countries produced more food per acre there than in others. He produced more not because he was bigger or better: the efficiency of conversion of food into productive work could not have been very different across the world. He was more productive because the land of the great tropical river valleys—valleys of the Ganges, Godavari, Huang Ho or Yang Tse—produced more grain per acre than, say, the plains of the Rhine or the Zambesi. More grain per acre meant less labour in ploughing and harvesting it, and hence higher human productivity.

Since work produced more in the fertile river valleys, everyone did not have to sow and reap, sow and reap. So there some could work less and live better than others. That is why the sites of great civilizations were also the sites of great empires—of large hierarchical systems where some worked while some ruled. Making other people work is laborious; that is why empires created bureaucracies. The great post-industrial empires inherited bureaucracies from pre-industrial times; that is why we have governments and businesses whose structures have so little to do with the work they have to do.

Those that could make others work could also live better than they; some lived much better. They could consume other things besides the essential food, clothes and shelter; they could enjoy palaces, fountains, furniture, dancing girls, fighting elephants, jewellery and fancy food. That is what we call civilization; pre-industrial civilizations grew where food producers produced more than their families ate.

It would be comfortable to enjoy the best things of life

without having to work for them. Many would like to do that; few could. Many tried to join the leisured class; few succeeded. Warfare was one form that the competition to join this class took. An aspirant joined an army; if it won, then he shared in its spoils. If it served a king, he would employ it, and pay it out of taxes. Thus the level of taxes determined the division of agricultural produce between those who produced it and those who lived off the producers. The agricultural tax in Mughal times was extremely high: something like two-thirds of the produce is reported to have been taken away. This is taken to be a measure of the oppressiveness of the regime. But it is also a measure of the productivity of the peasant of that time.

Now, this peasant would have ploughed his field as he does today. He would have walked to his field, carried his produce, winnowed his grain: in other words, he provided the motive power for production. But he would also have decided on which day to sow and on which to harvest, when to turn his bullocks around at the end of the field, what to do when one of them turned sick. In other words, he used and exercised intelligence, in the sense I used it in the previous section. Similarly, a jeweller would make a necklace to please a queen, a hakim would decide what medicine would revive her, a general would work out how to outwit a robber chieftain; they all exercised intelligence. Thus in pre-industrial times, as now, workers did a mixture of two things: they provided the motive power for production, and they exercised intelligence. In providing motive power they were helped by their draught animals; in exercising intelligence they were alone.

Newcomen and his steam engine changed all that; it was the first prime mover. Today, prime movers run on coal, oil or electricity and deliver motive power many times greater than the entire human work force. They began to replace human beings the day they arrived; by now they have replaced all the human beings many times over.

So what did human beings do? We might say that they were relieved of toil and drudgery; they could now exercise their intelligence. But if we count the activity of all the mechanical and electrical controllers today, we would come to the conclusion that the intelligence of human beings has also been outstripped many times over.

So how is it that any human is employed today? What is left for humans to do? One answer springs immediately to mind: they serve governments. They help governments collect compulsory levies and spend them. To these might be added two other classes. One is people who supervise the work of productive workers—managers for short. Today, productive outfits are themselves large like governments, and use bureaucracies to govern production. Another is the people who give money to governments and businesses and earn a return on it. So if they have invested enough, they can live on their investment income without working. As machines have displaced human beings, more human beings have moved into activities which do not involve providing motive power or guiding those who provide motive power.

It is true that people who serve governments or businesses or live in leisure are more numerous than in pre-industrial societies; these have been the growth industries even if the people they employ are not very industrious. It is also true that the proportion of people supplying motive power—manual workers—has fallen everywhere: it is falling in India, and manual workers are helped ever more in their work by prime movers. But it is not true that the proportion of workers, manual plus intellectual, is lower today than it was three hundred years ago; if anything, it is higher. For a larger proportion of the population works today. People are living longer, and a higher proportion of the years they have added to their lives is absorbed in work.

How is it then that as machines have destroyed human work on a massive scale, ever more human beings have found work? The answer lies in the rising standard of living. For the standard of living is just the obverse of human productivity. As human beings have been increasingly helped by prime movers and intelligent machines, they have produced more per head. That increased production has got translated into greater consumption and investment, into greater demand for goods and services; and that production has generated employment of humans.

Does this mean that everyone who is displaced by machines automatically finds a job? Obviously not. But no employer will replace a worker with a machine unless he saves cost. That cost saving will either go to him and increase his purchasing power, or go to his customers in the form of lower prices and increase theirs. As long as they spend their additional incomes, demand will increase for other goods and services which will be equal to the cost saving arising from the replacement of the worker. That demand will increase production of other things and employment in their production. If they do not spend their additional incomes, the additional demand will fall short of the cost saving. So any loss of jobs will not create exactly as many jobs somewhere else. One can imagine circumstances in which it will create more jobs than it destroys or destroy more jobs than it creates. But historically, mechanization has not led to reduced employment because increases in human productivity create jobs. Jobs available depend more on people's decisions to spend, lend or save their incomes than on the technology used.

Finance

Decisions to spend, lend or save—these are all financial decisions. How does money get involved in production, which is all about such things as goods and services?

Anyone can produce something without selling it: you may grow flowers on your window sill, or knit a pullover for your wife without demanding an immediate price. These activities produce something. They are too difficult to measure and are not normally included in measures of national product; but if you bought the pullover or the flower pot, the same activities would be included. In other words, production is for sale, even if it is only an intention to sell; and sale is the exchange of money—or a promise to pay money—for the produced good. The flow of production must be matched by a reverse flow of money or promises to pay. National income statisticians do make an exception if something that people produce and consume themselves is too important to leave out; for instance, they count the food farmers grow for themselves. But apart from this exception, measured production is production that is sold for money.

Money is anything people would accept for goods and services. If there were no money, a buyer would have to carry something more unwieldy—maybe pullovers or flower pots—when she goes marketing. She would approach the seller, who would look at her with a beady eye and start speculating what he could do with more flower pots—whether his hairdresser would take one, and whether a haircut would cost one pot or one and a quarter. Both buyers and sellers would waste so much time worrying about the possibility of using various things for exchange—called liquidity—that they would do little buying and selling. Money is a perfectly liquid asset. Its existence greatly multiplies exchanges, and production for exchange.

Money is universal buying power. It is so useful that those who get hold of it might never want to let go of it. If they hoard it, the reverse flow of money which brings forth production for sale would stop; people may continue to produce for themselves, but production would shrink. Conversely, they may spend more than they receive; in which case the value of production will increase.

But if you spend more money than you receive, you will soon run out of it, and then you will be in trouble. Readers of this book will generally not have experienced such trouble; I did once. There was a time when our government gave £8 in foreign exchange to all who wished to go abroad. I had come to India on holiday from Cambridge where I had a bank account. As I left Bombay, I bought £8 from the bank at the airport. I got to London, and wandered happily around for the day, expecting to take a train back to Cambridge. When I got to the railway station, I found that the last train had just left. Counting the money in my pocket, I walked around looking for a place where I could stay overnight for less than £8. I found one. The next morning, I got up, and started walking again, looking for a friend who would lend me money. All were away or unavailable, until I found one who said she was going to get her salary that afternoon; would I meet her at her office at 3 p.m. I walked to her office in the afternoon, took some money, and had my first meal in almost twenty-four hours. That is when I was convinced that money was the greatest invention of mankind.

The point of the story is that you can spend more than you receive—if you have someone who would allow you to use her money for a while. People cannot be prevented from spending less money than they receive; but as long as some other people spend that much more money than they receive, total expenditure on goods and services will continue undiminished. Savings out of income should be matched by expenditure on goods and services that is not out of income.

There is no way to ensure that excess savings will be invariably matched by excess expenditure; but their matching will be greatly helped if those who save hand over the money to those who want to spend more money than they have.

But savers are not such generous people; most of them are saving for old age, young kids or hard times. They would like to have their money back some time; and in the meanwhile they would like to earn something on the money they have given out. So they may lend the money until the time they expect to need it, and receive interest on it in the meanwhile. This is debt. Or they may take a share in someone's business, who may promise to give them a return depending on his profits; that is equity.

Suppose that you have saved a few thousand rupees, and you begin to look for someone who would take it for a few years and give you a good return. You go around your neighbourhood bazaar; none of the shopkeepers looks trustworthy. You go to Malabar Hill in Bombay. There the industrialists may look decent enough, but you cannot even get past their watchmen to have a chat. It would be a good idea to engage someone who would do the checking of people's trustworthiness—due diligence as they call it—for you. That is what the banks are supposed to do. They may not do it too well; almost a fifth of the government loans are irrecoverable. But anyway, vetting the borrower is their main job, and they charge a lot for it. They get 14 to 15 per cent from the borrowers, and give you 8 to 9 per cent on the average; they pocket the remaining 6 per cent, or close to two-fifths of what they earn.

What about equity, where the receiver of your money promises to give you a return based on his profits? Somehow it is unknown for such receivers to promise to give back your money after a fixed period. The idea is that by promising to share profits with you, they have made you a part-owner of the business. The only circumstances under which they would return your money is if they closed down their business; and even then, you would get paid only if something was left after paying off all the creditors.

Few people would be prepared to part with their money on those terms; and if they do, they will give their money only to people they know well and trust. Not much money would be available on those terms to businessmen who have great ideas or ability but no friends.

Hence has arisen the practice of raising equity by selling a large number of betting slips. Buying into the equity of a business is a gamble: a gamble on the success of the business, on the skill and honesty of the businessman, and on the line of business being well chosen. Many people would be prepared to place a small bet. To make the bet more attractive, markets are set up in which the betting slips, called share certificates, can be bought and sold. So then your money is not locked up until the business goes bankrupt; you can sell off your certificates at any time. Businesses that sell share certificates to raise capital are called public limited companies: public because anyone can buy into their ownership by buying their shares, and limited because your liability to their creditors is limited to what you have paid for your shares. If the company goes bankrupt and does not have enough assets to pay off all the creditors, they cannot come to you as a shareholder and demand to be paid. They are also called joint stock companies, on the ground that the stock they have is jointly owned by their shareholders.

Just as there are share certificates that can be bought and sold, so there are debt certificates, called debentures, in respect of which the company that raises them promises to repay the debt after some years. And there are share certificates, called preference shares, on which a company promises to pay a fixed rate of interest, but does not promise ever to repay what you paid for them.

Banks came first; they take your money, give you a return, and promise to pay you as much as you gave them. Companies came later; they sell you pieces of paper (or, nowadays, entries in a depository account, just like credits in a bank account) which you can sell to others in a market. Both these are very useful models, and many varieties of institutions have come up which combine them. For instance, pension funds take money from you and promise to give you a steady income when you get old. Insurance companies promise to pay you if you suffer certain misfortunes. Mutual funds take money from you, invest it in saleable securities—shares, debentures, government bonds etc.—and give you the market value of your investment whenever you want it. Venture capital funds invest your money in businesses that do not issue shares, in the hope that when these businesses grow and issue shares, the funds will make big profits on your investment for you. And these varied institutions offer a great variety of financial instruments.

What they all together achieve is to turn the savings of couch potato savers into productive assets. They help in the growth of the economy; and the more competitive and trustworthy they are, the more growth they will generate from people's savings. That is why the financial system is so central to the production process.

But the system is also prone to serious dangers. Rogues may take money from savers or from financial institutions and run away with it, or idiots may take it and squander it. The government may borrow money from them and waste it on unproductive activities. Since financial instruments—banknotes, share certificates etc.—are so cheap to print, they may be overissued, faked or duplicated.

The financial system needs to have good internal controls to prevent fraud and incompetence. And since not every bank or mutual fund will install such controls on its own, financial institutions have to be policed. Policing them is still an art that the financial police are learning; few get it entirely right.

MARKETS

We have come across a number of markets—for onions, sugar, grains, bonds etc. They are pretty commonplace phenomena; but they can generate uncommon emotions. Great virtues are attributed to the market system, and interference with them is condemned. At the same time, there are important players—governments, workers, even businessmen—who rail against them. What is it that makes them so emotive?

Before a producer can become a tycoon, he has to survive. And to survive he has to ensure four things. First, like all of us, he must have a cash balance. That means that his cash payments cannot exceed his receipts for long. Second, he must add value to the inputs he buys; the value of the goods and services he produces must exceed the value of the inputs he uses to make them. Third, he must pay off to their satisfaction the various claimants on that added value—workers, moneylenders, shareholders etc.—and be left with a profit for himself. Finally, profits add to the net assets of the business, and losses reduce them. If the assets are drawn down, a time may come when the businessman does not have enough assets to pay off all his debts. At that point, he must raise more capital if he is not to go bankrupt. The excess of his assets over his liabilities is his safety cushion; he must have as fat a cushion as he can. But he will also normally make bigger profits if his business grows, and to expand the business, he will be tempted to raise liabilities. Production is always risky; and growth generally involves assumption of more risk.

To do any of these things, he needs markets—markets in which he can sell his produce, buy his inputs, raise loans, issue shares, sell his assets. Markets are a great convenience to the businessman: they enable him to turn goods and services into money and vice versa. But they also determine whether the businessman passes the four tests above, and hence whether he survives and closes down his business. Those who have market dealings with a producer will be assessing the riskiness of doing so all the time. If he is at risk of defaulting on his debts, people will stop lending to him. Interest charged to business is invariably higher than interest charged to the government, which can always print money and hence is at no risk of default. And the risks borne by a producer can descend on his workers who may lose their jobs, his shareholders who may lose their dividends, or his creditors whose loans may turn sticky. Those at the receiving end of these risks will tend to blame the markets; and if they go and badger the government for protective action, so will the government.

Competition

So why do markets have admirers? They admire not so much markets, but competitive markets; and by competitive markets they mean markets in which the producer cannot influence the price he gets. He is so unimportant in the market that he can sell all he can produce at the price ruling in the market, and nothing at a price even slightly higher. If he is thus helpless in respect of the price, the only way he can raise his profits is by reducing his costs. All producers will be intent on reducing their costs and underselling their competitors; in these circumstances, their buyers will pay the lowest prices possible.

This is a powerful ideal. If all markets were competitive in this sense, all benefits of cost reduction and productivity increase would be passed on to consumers—instead of accruing to the producers and workers. They will spread throughout the economy, and not get stuck in those industries where the improvements are taking place. This is why, even where competitive conditions do not obtain, governments try to create them or mimic them. For instance, the regulator the British government has appointed for the denationalized electricity industry orders the industry to raise its prices at the rate of inflation minus 4 per cent; the idea is to force it to reduce costs. Similarly, when the US government hived off the local telephone business of Bell-AT&T, the telecommunications monopoly, to a number of smaller companies, it prohibited AT&T from competing with the Baby Bells for fifteen years. Only in India does the government protect the monopolies it owns in electricity, telecommunications, or railways and obstructs competitors even after it allows them in.

But the markets which come closest to this competitive ideal do not always produce ideal results. Many markets for agricultural commodities approximate to perfect competition. But you get garlic mixed up, of all sizes and qualities, fresh and desiccated; you cannot get the large, uniform, clean garlic bulbs you get in Europe. Cotton comes ingeniously adulterated; edible oil is sometimes so dangerous that it kills people. These products never improve; their producers continue to produce the same indifferent products decade after decade. Their profits are so meagre that they do not put money back into improvements; and price fluctuations and slim profit margins make their business so risky that no outside investor would be prepared to sink money into improving them.

So maybe it is better if some grit enters the gears of competition. There should not be so many competitors that none can make an attractive profit. At the same time, high profits should attract new producers from outside. The competition should be contestable: it should be possible to enter the market if producers make too much profit, but not too soon. This is an attractive possibility, but only a possibility. It is neither common, nor can it be made more common by policy.

But there is is a third type or model of competition which is more interesting and also more realistic. Pure competition assumes that competition occurs only in respect of price; in reality, competition occurs in a number of dimensions—price, product design, convenience of use, time of delivery, likelihood of breakdown, etc. Similarly, costs can be brought down by a number of devices—by means of faster machines, by lowering inventories, by reducing transport costs to the consumer, by reducing the likelihood of manufacturing defects etc. And producers are not simple creatures producing only one thing; they can spread risks and raise returns by producing a range of products, they can change processes of production, they can buy up other businesses or be bought up. Because they can act in so many different dimensions, they do not win or fail so quickly and inexorably as they would if they produced an identical product with very similar processes and sold it in the same market. There is greater uncertainty about the outcome of their actions. So investors are prepared to take bets on them by buying their shares, or cash their bets by selling the shares. In particular, if new knowledge is applied to the products or processes, it can only lead to gains. So producers in markets of this kind look for innovations, and investors back those who they think are good at innovation. That is how the product and capital markets serve to improve productivity and product quality in certain industrial economies.

As perceptions have changed, so have policies. Till about thirty years ago, competition among the many was regarded as ideal; at that time, simply splitting up big enterprises was considered a good thing. Especially in America, there was a certain atomistic evangelism. But once it is recognized that competition has many dimensions, it becomes much more difficult to formulate policy.

IV

The Lawful Robber

The Colombian government recently handed over a certain area of its country to a group of terrorists. They are to administer it. Young men with guns sit at street corners and keep the peace.

Why should the government do such a thing? Because they were in the same business. They both possess means of violence; they both intimidate. But the government claims a monopoly of violence; it cannot tolerate anyone challenging that monopoly. Colombia is a vast country, one third the size of India. It is extremely mountainous. Bogota, its capital, is 9000 feet high. Finding that I had a week on my hands in Bogota with nothing to do. I decided to go and see the Amazon, which Colombia touches to its south. I found there was no road down from the mountains to the river; I took a plane. The town of Leticia on the Amazon was a grid of three streets each way; the rest was equatorial jungle.

In such a country, the government monopoly of force does not extend very far. The first time I went to Bogota, I got out of the taxi on reaching the hotel and was taking out my money to pay the taxi driver, when he stopped me. He said, 'Place your suitcase between your legs and hold it tight before you take out your money.'

Another time, I had persuaded a local dignitary to address an international meeting I was holding in Manizales. He rang up a week before and asked to be excused. He said that he was very busy; while he was talking to someone he met at the airport, his briefcase had been stolen, and he had to rewrite all the papers. I told him that if the people I had invited to the meeting heard why he had cancelled, they would simply refuse to come to his hazardous country; so he agreed to come.

When he came, he told me the rest of the story. He had advertised in the newspaper saying that if the briefcase was returned to him, he would give a prize. He got a phone call asking him to go to a certain restaurant in the old city. In the restaurant, a man came to him with a little girl. The man said that he had not taken the briefcase, and that the thief would not come for obvious reasons. But if my friend gave him the money, he would come back immediately with the briefcase; in the meanwhile he would leave his daughter with my friend. So my friend sent him off with the money. Half an hour passed, but there was no sign of the intermediary. So my friend asked the girl, 'Where is your father?' The absconder was not her father, and was not seen again.

If that is how things work in the capital, the government writ in the remote parts of the country cannot be very effective; there, small farmers grow coca, which is then refined and smuggled into the United States, the world's biggest market. The US government does not allow the use of cocaine, and asks the Colombian government to stamp out coca cultivation. The Colombian government has tried for years; but cocaine business is highly profitable—profitable enough to enable its practitioners to maintain armies. After fighting these armies for years, the Colombian government decided that maintaining a monopoly of force was more important than putting down the terrorists, and so it handed over the local monopoly to a terrorist group.

Why is monopoly of force so important? Because it is believed that a monopoly will lead to less total violence than if a number of violent groups were operating in the same area. If there is an effective monopoly of force, all the violence will be that of the monopoly; if that monopoly does not perpetrate violence pointlessly or in its own interest—if it seriously tries to minimize violence—then it will actually minimize it. If it surely and quickly punishes those who indulge in violence, it will minimize the chances that anyone else will be violent. That is the theory: that peace is maximized by an effective monopoly that works to minimize violence. That monopoly is government. Not all governments have an effective monopoly of violence; nor do all avoid wanton violence. But all governments claim to try. They claim to enforce order by law.

People obviously value peace; they would be prepared to pay for it. But if everyone bought as much order as he could afford, there would be no monopoly of force. A tycoon may employ a private army, a small businessman may keep one guard, and the poor would be at the mercy of the many private forces. We did have that condition until the British enforced a monopoly of violence in India. At the end of the eighteenth century, those who could afford them carried arms; traders travelled in convoys with armed guards, and sheltered at night in fortified serais; kings built fortresses around towns, within which all who could afford it lived. The structure of the havelis of that time, with strong outer walls and a single gate, and an inner courtyard into which all rooms opened, tells the same story.

Nor would it do if the government had a monopoly of

force, but everyone bought its services when he liked. Again, the rich would buy more services than the poor; and even they would not be able to anticipate always when they might need the services of the police. They would engage the police when they had a wedding and the guests were expected to turn up in all their finery; but they could not be sure when robbers might strike otherwise. Hence, if there was a market for security, there would be less security overall than if there was a monopoly which supplied security irrespective of how much security anyone wanted.

The security force would cost something, and must be paid for. Since its services must not be sold piecemeal, they must be paid by a compulsory contribution from those protected. That is taxation. Again, a government cannot tolerate competitors extorting compulsory levies; if it did, its own collections would suffer. Monopoly of violence and monopoly of taxation: these are the core characteristics of a government.

Peace is not the only good which a market cannot efficiently provide; there are a number of goods—called public goods—like it. Their characteristic is that if they are provided by one person, they benefit others without their having to pay for it. Traffic management is an example. Without traffic lights and policemen, there would be chaos at busy crossings; but if some daring samaritan set himself up on a pedestal in the middle and started directing the traffic, everyone would heave a sigh of relief. Conversely, there are goods which, if provided by someone for his own benefit, harm others. For instance, villagers in coastal villages no doubt get relief, if not joy, when they visit the beaches every morning and squat; but their daily enjoyment leaves the beaches unusable by bathers. Without denying the villagers' need to squat, there are ways of making both them and bathers happier, but they involve compelling both to change their preferences.

Thus a monopoly institution is necessary to provide public goods; it must be financed from compulsory contributions. That monopoly is the government. But if it has full freedom to extract contributions, there is every danger that it will extract too much; if it is to determine how much of common goods to supply, it may well supply too little at too high a cost. Where goods are sold in markets, competition curbs producers' tendency to charge too much or deliver too little. How can such a tendency be curbed in the government? There is no good answer to this question. There is a conventional answer, but it can certainly be improved.

ROBBERY

The government of India rules over a country of 1 billion people spread over 360,000 square kilometres. Most countries are smaller. But they are getting bigger—ceding powers to supranational institutions. This process is happening before our eyes in Europe, where integration has gone so far that it is irreversible. Common markets have emerged—Association of South-East Asian Nations (ASEAN) in Asia to our east, North American Free Trade Area (NAFTA) in North America, and Mercosur in Latin America.

Countries used to be much smaller; indeed, there was a time when countries were no bigger than villages or communities. In those times, the most popular taxation was taxation of foreigners. It was best to raid a neighbouring village or country and carry back everything portable—crops, cattle, furniture. Until a few years ago, it was still the custom among the people of Papua New Guinea to raid villages in the next valley, mainly for pigs and women.

Nor is the custom confined to primitive people. After World War I, the Allies took away 'reparations' from the Germans in the form of entire factories. In World War II, the Soviets took away old paintings from the art galleries of Germany; both sides are still negotiating gingerly about their return.

But this form of taxation is more in the nature of betting. A village may have to pay taxes as often as it receives them, depending on who raids whom and who wins the ensuing battle. And the tax may have to be paid in the form not only of pigs but also of lives and broken legs. The risks increased dramatically with the advent of modern arms; today, the tax may be in the form of millions dead and entire cities destroyed. As warfare has become more destructive, states have grown in size, and war for profit has virtually disappeared.

There are not many ways of taxing foreigners peacefully. Some people think that taxing imports is a way of taxing foreigners. But they are wrong. India's share of world trade is 0.5 per cent; in terms of trade, the rest of the world would hardly notice if India disappeared tomorrow. If India imposes an import duty, the exporter abroad is not going to reduce the price; it is more likely that he will charge an unchanged price and that the Indian importer will pay the duty. Similarly, the central government charges a luxury tax on bills of expensive hotels on the assumption that mostly foreigners will pay; local governments levy similar taxes. Actually, international tourists are most price-sensitive; if a holiday in India gets more expensive, they will go to Thailand or Indonesia.

Wherever warfare subsided and stable governments emerged, they invariably taxed agriculture. Agriculture was by far the largest industry, and farmers could not run away. But taxing crops required a large and alert bureaucracy. The tax had to be collected in a short period, just when the crops were harvested; and it had to bear some relation to the crop, so the crop had to be estimated if not actually measured and divided between the farmer and the government.

So governments looked for easier things to tax, and found a lucrative source in moving goods. If goods were being taken from one place to another, they could be taxed at a point on the way; bridges and fords were favourite points for such robbery. The tradition continues in our octroi duties today; trucks are stopped on the way into a city and made to pay tax. Even easier to tax were goods that could not move, namely property.

Aged principles

But if it is too heavy, taxation defeats itself. It leads to a contraction of the tax base. Heavy land taxes will force farmers to run away, octroi will force travelling traders out of business; and the heavier the tax, the more likely it is to be evaded. Hence the British developed the practice of taxing a lot of things at low rates. That practice is reflected in the seventh Schedule of our Constitution, which gives thirteen taxes that only the centre can levy and twenty that the states can levy.

In the past fifty years, the realization has dawned all over the world that all taxes will be paid out of someone's income, whatever they are levied on. So then income might as well be the principal base of taxation. This can take two forms. One is the income generated by enterprises—their value added; value added tax is the rage these days. The other is income received by individuals. Its taxation permits adjusting the tax to their capacity to pay; the rich can be taxed more than the poor. The third is a hybrid of the value added tax and the personal income tax. It is corporate or business income tax. It is levied on enterprises like value added tax; but it is levied on profits, or business income. Finally, there are taxes on assets: on real property or personal wealth. Taxes on transactions and on movement of goods have gone out of fashion. Taxes on trade are considered destructive of production; for instance, average customs duties in industrial countries have fallen to single digit percentages.

But taxation in India is still mired in an earlier age. The Constitution reserves a few, lucrative taxes for the centre—customs duties on imports, excise duties on production, corporate and personal income. But it has to give a high proportion of the taxes to the states. The states can levy many taxes, but most yield very little; so they have come to rely increasingly on sales taxes, which are very similar to the centre's excise duties. They have also begun to encroach on the centre's taxes. For instance, West Bengal taxes the profits of tea companies, but calls it land revenue; many states levy primitive income taxes but call them professions taxes. The states also levy taxes on transactions in property and financial assets.

They both have forgotten the principle that taxation should be moderate; the higher it is, the more people are tempted to evade it. And if tax collectors are poorly paid, they will help people evade taxes, and in the process help themselves. The centre and the states together collect about a fifth of the national income in taxes. This is low compared to other countries; industrial countries collect a half or more of national incomes, and a number of Asian and Latin American countries collect between a quarter and a third. But no one knows how much the Indian tax collectors collect for themselves; all we know is that the attraction of tax collection services has increased, and that young people fight to get into them rather than into the foreign service or the administrative service. If the tax collectors' take is included, our taxes may be no lower than in comparable developing countries.

Manmohan Singh believed in moderate taxes. When he became finance minister, he reduced tax rates. He also extended value added taxation. The results were strange. Although income tax rates were greatly reduced, income tax revenue increased as a proportion of national income. The proportion of revenue from production taxes, on the other hand, went down. My own guess is that income tax revenue went up because there are very few income tax officers and millions of income taxpayers; in commodity taxation, on the other hand, there are many more tax collectors and fewer taxpayers. So more income tax reached the treasury, whereas excise officers made better deals with taxpayers and intercepted more revenue.

So efficiency in taxation is not only a matter of their level or design; it also depends on the terms on which tax officers are recruited, appointed and controlled. This relates not only to tax officers, but to all government employees, and is best discussed later when we come to the design of the government. But as far as the design is concerned, the arrangements in the Constitution have worked badly, and need to be changed.

A simple design

It is a bad idea to levy a great variety of taxes on many bases; the number of bases has shrunk all over the world, and would shrink eventually to four. The first is production, and the tax base is value added. The trend is towards a value added tax. The next is income tax—that is, on the part of added value that goes to individuals. The idea of taxing income is that richer individuals should pay higher tax. The third is wealth. Wealth taxation was very popular after the War, but has declined since, largely because of the difficulty of valuing wealth. But there is no such difficulty about real property, which is taxed everywhere by local authorities. And the last base is persons. Poll taxes have had a poor reputation. Margaret Thatcher levied one in Britain to finance local authorities, but it was so unpopular that it had to be withdrawn. A general, national poll tax is not such a good idea unless there is a guarantee that everyone would receive enough income to pay it. But in India, where people are moving into towns and using their infrastructure, there is nothing wrong in making them pay a tax per head for using it. It would be a membership subscription for living in a town.

If the number of taxes is limited and there is a multiplicity of governments—central, state, local—it would be wrong to allocate each tax to only one level. Property and poll taxes are best left to local authorities; in which case the centre and the states are left with only value added and income taxes. In that case both should be able to levy either tax. Although they may levy separate taxes on the same base, it would be a waste if they had separate tax collecting mechanisms. Nor is it necessary to have separate collection authorities for value added and income taxes. Historically, there have been for commodity taxation and income taxation. But value added tax is a tax on all incomes, not on commodities; it should be calculated from annual profit and loss accounts, and collected by the same machinery. This machinery may be told by the centre to levy a certain rate of tax, and a state may ask it to collect an additional tax on value added or income in its own boundaries. In Canada, there is only one income tax return. There are two parts in it, one to calculate the tax owing to the federal government and the other to the state government; the two are added up and paid with a single cheque.

Thus the tax system can be considerably simplified. There would be a single value added tax levied by the centre, and a single VAT within each state. The sum of the two would be collected once a year on the basis of audited accounts from every business. Similarly, there would be only one exemption limit and one set of income brackets, on which income tax may be levied by the centre and the states; the sum would be collected from individuals by a single authority. Within each local authority there would be a single poll tax and a single rate of property tax, which would be based on indices of property value in various localities, and not on the value of each particular property.

Finally, those services that the government sells—for instance, property registration, education or medical services—should be priced at cost, and the pricing should be non-discriminatory: one consumer should not have to pay more than another. If the government thinks that people should have more of the services than they would if the services were provided at cost, it should give them a subsidy—and the subsidy should come out of the government's budget.

GENEROSITY

A government lives on compulsory contributions it forces subjects to pay. If money can be raised simply by sending a demand note, what is to prevent the government from raising too much? From ruining taxpayers? And if the government provides certain services free—for instance, security, or roads—how is their supply to be determined? Is every case of theft and fraud to be pursued till solved, or are the police to be selective for the sake of limiting expenditure?

It was to resolve problems like this that democracy was invented. Taxation may be called the mother of democracy. There was a time when kings claimed an unlimited right of taxation. The right was also exercised quite arbitrarily. For instance, the noblemen whom the state enriched were not taxed, while the poor farmers bore the brunt of taxation. The protests of those taxed led to the calling of the House of Commons in Britain and the Etats General in France. The Boston Tea Party, in which the American subjects began their revolution against the English king by throwing tea out of ships, was against taxation without representation. Democratic constitutions make government expenditure conditional upon approval by an elected assembly.

The theory is that since it is not possible to get the consent of every taxpayer, it is obtained from representatives they elect. At the same time, they are shown a plan of expenditure out of the tax revenue and would approve it. The approval is valid for a year, after which it has to be renewed. This is what annual budgets are about. To ensure that the expenditure does not exceed approvals, there is a finance ministry to keep accounts, and its officers in other ministries to keep their expenditures within their budgets; and there is an audit after the event by the Comptroller and Auditor General.

The question is, whose representatives? Originally it was representatives of taxpayers. The ballot in Britain was restricted to property-owners; there were similar restrictions in other countries. But if people should not be taxed without their consent, nor should they be sent to die in battle; and most who died in battle were not property owners. Thus came progressive extension of the right to vote; women were given the right in Britain less than eighty years ago. Today, it would be heresy to say that universal suffrage is a bad idea.

But universal suffrage has tilted the balance in parliaments against taxpayers and in favour of those who benefit from government expenditure. Taxes invariably rise in wartime; and when they rise, they become more progressive. They rose to extraordinary levels during World War II. They should have come down after the War, but in most countries, parliaments found peacetime uses for the tax revenue. The uses were all laudable: health, education, old age pensions, unemployment benefit etc. But these were not public goods; they could be supplied by private producers. If purely private operations did not result in high enough consumption of medical care, education, or insurance, they could be subsidized. But the governments of industrial countries went instead into the direct provision of these services. That is how they today appropriate more than two-fifths of their national incomes in taxation. The same process of overtaxation and overreach of government occurred in India as well; but here there are some additional problems.

The cult of the giftless amateur

The members of Indian legislatures are incapable of controlling government revenue and expenditure; they have neither the training nor the interest. Typically, very little of the budget session of Parliament or of legislative assemblies is actually devoted to discussing the budget proposals; almost all are passed at the last minute without discussion. Nor is this true of the budget only; almost all the legislation throughout the year is passed with little discussion, and when there is discussion—for instance of the Patent Bill—there is little understanding. The level of the legislators' comprehension is reflected in the attendance in the houses. Most of the time, fewer than twenty-five members out of the 543 are present. The only time when almost everyone is present is the question hour and the zero hour; and the issues raised in those hours are mostly local constituency-based issues.

This problem of lack of expertise arises in the parliaments of other countries also. To deal with it, they have adopted various devices.

The most common device is parliamentary committees. They review impending laws or study issues. They are a device to compress the huge, unwieldy legislature into a small group of more competent and interested members, to get more detailed information from the government and to bring in outside expertise. They are used in India as well. There are two permanent committees of Parliament—the Estimates Committee and the Committee on Public Enterprises. There are Standing Committees attached to each ministry. There are Joint Parliamentary Committees on occasional issues like fertilizer pricing in 1992 or the bank scam in 1993.

But the body of talent available is so small that it is not even enough to man committees. Committees sit for long periods and produce little value addition at the end of it. They are too large; there are so many parties in Parliament that a committee representing all the major ones is inevitably large. And what emerges from the committees still falls short of legislation. In the United States, committees of the Senate or the House of Representatives actually draft legislation; in Britain, their reports are almost directly translated into legislation. That almost never happens in India, because committees cannot marshal enough expertise.

Another device, employed in Britain, is the shadow cabinet. The opposition party chooses a competent member to concentrate on one particular ministry and become an expert on its affairs; he or she routinely leads when debate turns to that ministry. This too has never worked in India; parties do not have enough competent people to form a shadow cabinet, and debate in legislatures invariably turns to very general topics.

A third device is an upper house; in Britain, judges, lawyers, professionals and experts are given peerages so that they can sit in the House of Lords and contribute their expertise. Our state legislatures have largely abolished upper houses. The upper house of Parliament is elected by state legislators; although its standard of competence is better on average than that of the lower house, it is still not sufficient.

No visible means of support

Political parties in democratic countries are typically coalitions of powerful lobbies. A common pattern is a rightist and leftist party; this pattern emerged in the early days of industrialization and has held on through a century or longer. Even where the left-right divide is blurred, lobbies coalesce to form parties. It is the lobbies that raise finance for the parties they support.

In India too, there are lobbies behind parties, but they do not finance parties: they expect parties to finance them. A typical Indian party has a feudal structure; it consists of local gangs following local leaders. The numbers involved in politics are very large. A local leader keeps his followers together by bringing them benefits at the cost of the state.

A favourite way of doing this in the early days of independence was through distribution of scarce resources. For instance, there was a severe shortage of corrugated iron sheets. The minister of steel issued allocation permits to politicians' nominees; they shared the black market profits with the politicians. A recent example of the same sort is the permits for petrol pumps issued by Captain Satish Sharma to the kin and friends of Congress politicians when he was petroleum minister—permits which were later cancelled by the Supreme Court.

Another way was to create dual markets, so that a beneficiary could buy at a low price and sell at a high price. The typical example of this is foodgrain rationing. Here, in theory, subsidized foodgrains are given in small quantities to the poor and deserving. Studies have shown that a large proportion of the poor have no access to the rations, that the subsidies conveyed per head are so small that most would not bother to claim them, and that a large proportion of the foodgrains is diverted to the open market. A similar dual market operates in education; politicians or their friends set up colleges and receive subsidies. Dual markets of this sort create profits for politicians and their friends to intercept.

A third is government expenditure. Contracts are given to people with political influence; loans and subsidies are channelled through committees where politicians have influence. Jobs in the government are given or sold to supporters.

A fourth is interception of government revenue. Politicians get their nominees appointed to key revenue collectors' posts. The collectors make deals with taxpayers, and share the profits with their patrons.

The last way does not involve interception of government expenditure or revenue, but sale of government power—for instance, power to punish criminals, or power to register property transfers.

Partial remedies

It is possible to think of a number of ways of preventing

political corruption, but they are all partial. The liberals' view is that if government controls and subsidies are abolished, they would eliminate politicians' rents. This is what Manmohan Singh tried in the early 1990s; but the politicians stopped him before he got far. Even if controls and subsidies are abolished, there is no way of abolishing government contracts, or the police.

Another suggested reform is state funding of elections. The Narasimha Rao government had placed government expenditure of Rs 1 crore in each constituency at the discretion of the member of Parliament (the BJP government raised it to Rs 2 crores). Manmohan Singh had proposed that the government should instead fund the parties in proportion to their votes in the last election. He did not succeed.

The idea behind this proposal is that politicians corrupt themselves because of the cost of elections. This is partly true; but politicians have more down-to-earth reasons to be corrupt: corruption is profitable. The Election Commission has done much to reduce election expenses—reduced the period of campaigning, banned certain types of expenditure, and required audit of parties' accounts. But even if elections cost nothing, politicians would have good reasons to be corrupt.

A game for two teams

What then is the solution? It must achieve a number of things together: it must reduce the labour-intensity of politics, it must bring forth more competent candidates, and it must increase the chances of a party's coming to power, so that it is tempted to serve the interests of the majority of the people.

My solution is a system of proportional representation

with a very high cut-off point—say 20 per cent. A party getting fewer than 20 per cent of the votes would get no seats at all. A party getting more than 20 per cent would get seats in proportion to its votes. It would have to put forward a list of candidates before the election; as many of them, starting from the top of the list, would be elected as the party gets seats.

Provided the cut-off point is high enough, only two parties will get seats; if the cut-off point were 50 per cent, only one party at most will get into the legislature. Proportional representation will give an advantage to parties against individuals; funding of parties is not corruption, whereas funding of individuals may be. And to win, a party will have to get votes from all over the country. Parties will put up candidates who are well known throughout the country, and who therefore are likely to have a track record. It will also put up a balanced list, in which all major interests and groups would find representation.

Once the number of parties is reduced to two or three, parties and individuals will not be able to get into Parliament by advocating the interests of a locality or caste; the parties will have to attract a national vote, and will have to focus on national issues. On each issue they will have to calculate whether the position they take will attract or alienate more voters; they will thus be drawn to take positions the majority supports. All parties will move towards the political centre. In Britain, Tony Blair brought the Labour Party back to power after seventeen years in 1996 by stealing Tory policies; in 1998, Gerhard Schröder brought his party in Germany back to power after eighteen years by taking its stance closer to the centre. In India itself, the BJP came to power in 1998 by abandoning extreme stances of Hindutva and swadeshi and adopting the traditional ideological clothes of the Congress. Political competition leads to less extremism and more responsibility if parties have a reasonable chance of coming to and staying in power; and the smaller the number of parties, the greater the chance each has of coming to power.

Representing other interests

The present political system gives the vote to all adults; they are the electorate. Within this system of adult suffrage, there is an attempt to give representation to geographical areas. This is done in two ways. The country is divided into constituencies, each of which elects a member of Parliament. And the upper house is elected by the members of state legislatures.

There is, however, one interest that is not represented in the legislature, namely the taxpayer. And yet, if he is going to finance the state, he should have a voice in deciding how the money he parts with is spent. There is a simple way of giving him a voice: half the seats in the legislatures should be elected by personal income tax payers. Each should have a vote in proportion to the tax he pays. Election of taxpayers' candidates should also be based on proportional representation. The election would be very simple. An additional page in the income tax return would act as the ballot paper.

Just now, all ordinary matters require a simple majority in a legislature, and constitutional changes require a three-quarters majority. This can continue. But money bills, involving taxation, expenditure and borrowing, should require a majority of the taxpayers' representatives alone.

Proportional representation and a two-party system will not give representation to the interests of regions and small groups as much as the present system does. The solution to this problem is to have a larger number of states. The present states were set up when the British empire was dissolved; they were organized to give a state to each language group. It is an advantage if a government can communicate to its people. But that does not mean that there cannot be a number of states speaking the same language; there actually are a number of Hindi-speaking states. The ideal structure of a state is a city surrounded by hinterland which it can service and from which it can draw supplies. It would be best served if all cities with a population of over half a million in 2001 were made capitals of states; that would give us about fifty cities. That may leave some states with a very large area; they may be divided up into a number of states with smaller capitals. A hundred states would still be quite manageable. Their legislatures can continue to elect an upper house.

Interstate transfers

Finally, what is to be done with the transfers from the centre to the states? The Constitution built in an elaborate mechanism for such transfers; a new finance commission is set up every five years and it divides the centre's revenue between it and the states. In addition, the Planning Commission presides over loans and grants from the centre to the states. By now, the burden of the states' debt to the centre is so huge that the centre has to give them fresh loans every year to enable them to repay their past loans. Even then some of them cannot meet their obligations; for instance, they do not pay for their purchases of electricity and coal from the central companies.

This is an inherently unhealthy relationship and should be severed; neither the centre nor the states should subsidize or lend to one another. Once the states are allowed to levy the same taxes as the centre, one reason for such transfers—that the centre's taxes are more lucrative than the states'—would disappear. The other reason is to transfer money from the richer to the poorer states. The aim should be to transfer money not to the state governments, but to the people of those states; and the money should be given not in the form of subsidies, but of public investment. When East Germany collapsed and merged itself with West Germany, West Germany did not dole out subsidies to the poorer citizens of East Germany. Instead, it invested in the infrastructure of East Germany—roads, railways, telecommunications—to bring them up to West German standards. It has spent more every year on East Germany than the total international development aid being given by all donor countries. But it has used it to improve the productive capacity of the East Germans. In India too, we should have the same standard of public services from Leh to Trichy, from Junagadh to Imphal, instead of giving enormous subsidies to Nagaland and Kashmir on which the local politicians and bureaucrats flourish.

Controlling the courtiers

A system of proportional representation would bring more eminent persons into legislatures, increase the control of parties on individual politicians, and reduce the scope for political corruption. A two-party system would give stability to parties and induce them to pursue long-term popularity. Representation for taxpayers in legislatures would bring back responsibility into the management of public finances.

But the work of the government would still be done by bureaucrats. They can still waste money or be corrupt. Even today, corruption is mostly bureaucratic. Far more people are oppressed by the corruption of the sales tax officer, the electricity billing clerk or the telephone linesman than they are by the local member of legislative assembly. How are the bureaucrats to be made to deliver maximum value added for the expenditure?

The problem is the same as when the British government took over the government of India from the East India Company in 1857. At that time too there was rampant corruption in the bureaucracy. The corruption went up to the directors of the East India Company, who used the Company's ships to trade on their own account, and sold jobs in the civil service and the army.

To stamp out this corruption, the British government completely replaced the senior bureaucracy. Instead of making grace-and-favour appointments, it recruited by examination. It gave its civil servants such high salaries that they could live like minor princes. It created vertical hierarchies, so that the civil servants could look forward to promotion from Under Secretary to Joint Secretary, Additional Secretary and Secretary. And it expected these civil servants to keep their juniors working efficiently and honestly.

These reforms certainly succeeded in cleaning up the higher civil service, But they failed overall. They did not clean up the lower civil service. B.K. Nehru, in his autobiography, recounts how he used to dispense justice as a fresh member of the Indian Civil Service: he used to follow the guidance of his clerk, whom he discovered to be taking money from the litigants. Today we have the same civil service, but it does not even try to limit corruption and wrongdoing. Its deterioration has much to do with the domination of politicians; but reform of politicians will not be enough to improve the civil service. Both the composition of the civil service and its work have to be changed.

First, the recruitment into the civil service. Originally, the civil service examination was in humanities and literary subjects—English, history, classical languages. The idea was to choose people with communication skills and a broad knowledge. The government works on information; communication is the core of its activity. Now, however, candidates are allowed to take almost any subject. A large proportion of those who get in take 'scoring' subjects—science, engineering, medicine and mathematics—most of which have nothing to do with administration.

This aimless examination needs to be replaced by one in subjects essential for running the government. There are six: English, a local language, accountancy, law, economics and mathematics. If the government begins to recruit those educated in these subjects, universities will begin to offer a degree which consists of only these. Just as, fifty years ago, a BA degree was the passport to all jobs, this new bachelor's degree in practical arts will become the entry point to all administrative and managerial jobs, in the government and outside.

But the primary entrance qualification should not be this examination; it should be work experience. Only young people with at least three years' experience should be eligible for being taken into the government. This would ensure two things. First, the entry salaries in the government would have to match those prevalent in the rest of the economy; the vicious circle of low salaries and low quality would be broken. Second, the high cost of junior staff and the possibility that they may leave the government will compel a concern about their productivity and their work satisfaction. Just now, the junior staff members are recruited only for filing, typing and such mindless jobs, and have poor chances of promotion. Hence once they join the government, they cease to learn or improve. They fall into a low-productivity routine, and their interest shifts to office politics—manipulating appointments, transfers, promotions, collecting bribes, controlling access to information. To break these patterns of behaviour, it is necessary to recruit more able clerks, and have greater mobility amongst them.

This mobility can be ensured by stipulating that if a junior employee does not take the entrance examination and join the senior civil service by the age of thirty, he must leave. At that stage, the opinion of his superiors, the members of the senior civil service with whom he has worked, would also matter. The procedure would be that he would complete a three-year contract; at that stage, on the basis of the superior's recommendation, the government would allow him to take the examination, or renew his contract (as long as he is under thirty), or relieve him.

The recruits to the senior civil service would be thirty when they join. They would be given a ten-year contract. At its end, they may be relieved, or on their superiors' recommendation, be given another ten-year contract; at the end of that contract, they may get a third ten-year contract. At sixty they would retire. Thus, there would be only three levels in the senior civil service. The breaks at the end of every ten years would ensure that the size of the senior civil service would match the work to be done. Just now, every civil service is so overmanned that it has appropriated many jobs which are not its (for instance, vice chancellorships of universities) and created unnecessary jobs (in government corporations and agencies).

Tailoring the size of the civil service to the work will achieve three objects. First, it will provide everyone with a challenging job. Second, it will deprive politicians of the opportunities of choosing pliant civil servants to work with, relegating the rest to the backwaters. Cooperative civil servants are indispensable to politicians who specialize in corruption and impropriety. If there are just as many senior civil servants available as there are jobs, there will still be some matching of politicians and civil servants. But if a civil servant is not given one of the available posts, he will have to be prematurely dismissed and someone prematurely promoted, with the accompanying stink and questioning. Finally, if civil servants are dismissed and recruited from outside at the ages of forty and fifty, their salaries will have to be comparable with those in the private sector.

The proliferation of ministers and bureaucrats has also led to a proliferation of ministries. Many of them oversee enterprises that should not be owned by the government at all. Some have regulatory functions that are better performed by quasi-judicial authorities. The number of essential ministries is very small; it corresponds to the public goods that the government must supply—external relations, defence, internal peace, economic management, infrastructure management and social services. These may be divided into departments to make the work manageable for individual civil servants. These civil servants would in effect be managers of an activity. They would be given a budget for the activity, and would have full freedom to choose the staffing.

This is the answer to the question: how is the government's tendency to tax too much or to waste the money it raises to be restrained? Its temptation to tax too much must be curbed by the presence of taxpayers' representatives in legislative bodies. The money the legislatures authorize must be allocated through the budgetary process between ministries and departments, which will be managed by a small number of senior civil servants. The budget will also specify what they are expected to achieve during the year. They would have full freedom to spend the budget, including the freedom to hire and fire junior staff.

MACROECONOMIC POLICY

Its monopoly of force gives the government considerable power to interfere with the economy. This power attracts busybodies as honey attracts bees. Amongst them are economists. Many economists dream of becoming advisers to governments; they spend considerable time writing about policies in the hope that some government will implement their ideas. They all believe in a rational government that has the wisdom to see the sensibility of what they propose.

But far more numerous, active and influential than economists are interest groups. Most want the state to use the government for their own gain. Some want to use it to punish their enemies, others to escape the punishment that is lawfully theirs. Still others want to use it to realize grandiose dreams. My most vivid memory from my days in the government was of a man who collared me whenever he could and tried to persuade me to build a new capital for India.

It is only right that people should be able to influence policy and persuade their representatives; the responsiveness of the government is an index of democracy. But it is equally important that the government should not be a weapon in the hands of those who want to benefit themselves or punish others. The more intrusive the government, the more people will want to seize control and to prevent others from seizing it; the more bitter and unscrupulous political conflict will be. It is not enough that the political system be democratic; it must also be neutral between interests. This is the object of a two-party system based on proportional representation: parties in such a system will have to seek the broadest support and will be least swayed by special interests.

If the neutrality of the state is achieved, economic policy will be reduced to its essentials. These are to fix two quantities and two prices that only the government can fix. The quantitities are money supply and the foreign exchange reserves of the government. The prices are the base interest rate and the exchange rate.

Money supply

The government has a monopoly of currency issue. This is not an absolute monopoly, for there are substitutes for currency. The most important is bank deposits; a cheque or draft, though not issued by the government, is as much money as a currency note. A money substitute of growing importance is credit taken on credit cards. But the government can control the supply of all these kinds of money, by issuing money or by borrowing or lending—that is, exchanging money for debt.

Just now, the government spends so much more than it gets in revenue that it has to keep borrowing. It has already borrowed so much that it has to borrow in order to repay. It forces banks to lend to the state governments by specifying the statutory liquidity ratio—by laying down that they must invest a quarter of their deposits in state government securities. It similarly forces pension funds and insurance companies to buy government bonds. If that is not enough, it persuades the banks to buy more securities; since the central government owns most of the banks, the Reserve Bank of India, its treasurer, has no difficulty persuading them. But the more it borrows, the more interest it would have to pay. So it meets a substantial part of its needs by issuing money. Thus the growth of money supply is that part of the government's excess spending which cannot be financed by borrowing; the Reserve Bank, which is a part of the government, sells securities to itself, and pays the government for them in money which the government then spends.

If, however, we get parties and governments that take a long view, they will begin to keep spending within revenue; and if we get a civil service which is judged on its performance, it will begin to maximize the output of government services from the money it is given to spend. Then the Reserve Bank will not need to print government securities, put them in its own pocket and pay the government for them. There will be no surplus of securities to issue money against.

Then, if it wants to increase money supply, it will have to buy some other financial asset. It will either buy private securities, and thus give credit to productive activities, or foreign exchange, either earned by exporters or brought in by foreign investors.

Central banks lend either to very respectable financial institutions or to blue-chip companies at low rates of interest; the interest rate they charge becomes the floor for all other interest rates. Hence by borrowing and lending in the market, the Reserve Bank can set all interest rates, and determine the cost of finance for productive activities. It does so now as well, but it has to borrow so much for the government that it has to pay high interest rates; the high interest rates make many private investments unprofitable. But if the Reserve Bank were not so burdened by the need to finance government deficits, it would set the interest rates as required by the state of the economy. If there is not enough investment and the economy is not expanding fast enough, it would lower interest rates. If demand is expanding too fast and prices are rising, it would raise interest rates. This is how interest rates are steered by the Federal Reserve Board in the US or by the Bank of England.

Exchange rate

The exchange rate is the price of the local currency in terms of a foreign currency—for instance, the price of dollars in terms of rupees. The Reserve Bank can influence the exchange rate in two ways. One is by raising or lowering interest rates. A change in the interest rate will change the rate of return on financial investments, and will attract money from abroad or make it leave the country. The other is by buying or selling foreign currency for local currency.

The exchange rate is not simply the price of a currency. Exporters receive their export proceeds in foreign currencies, which they then convert into dollars; similarly importers buy foreign currencies to be able to pay for imports. So exporters' profits and importers' costs are influenced by the exchange rate.

By depreciating the rupee—that is, by reducing its value in terms of foreign currencies—the Reserve Bank can increase the rupees exporters would get for a certain dollar value of exports; that is, it can make exports more profitable, and thus stimulate them. At the same time, it can make imports more costly, and discourage them. By depreciation, therefore, it can improve the balance of payments, and increase the protection of domestic products against imports. But depreciation will increase the rupee value of both imports and exports and tend to raise prices. Conversely, by appreciating the rupee, the Reserve Bank can discourage exports, encourage imports, intensify the competition of imports against domestic products, and dampen inflation. Changing the exchange rate is the most neutral way of changing the terms of competition between domestic and foreign goods; it is better than levying import duties or export taxes on particular goods.

At present, the government spends so much more than it receives that the Reserve Bank has to finance a great deal of the excess by issuing money. When people come to hold larger money balances they begin to spend more; if they spend more and production cannot rise to match the expenditure, prices rise. And when domestic prices rise, exports become more expensive and tend to come down; imports become cheaper relative to domestic produce and are stimulated. Thus the government's compulsive borrowing causes inflation, and tends to worsen the balance of payments.

A balance of payments deficit may be partly financed by net inflow of money coming in from abroad for investment. If it is not so financed, then people will buy foreign exchange from the Reserve Bank to make the excess payments abroad, and the Reserve Bank's foreign exchange reserves will fall. If the Reserve Bank gets worried about its foreign exchange reserves and wants to conserve them, it will devalue the rupee. That is the connection between government deficit, inflation, and depreciation of the rupee. But if the government ceases to run a deficit, the Reserve Bank can manage the exchange rate so as to regulate inflation, give or withdraw protection to domestic industry, influence its exchange reserves, and control money supply. It is a difficult task, but at least the Reserve

Bank would be able to make a policy in the interests of the economy, and not the interests of the government.

TIME TO STOP

By now I have collected many reasons to stop. I have wandered far from my original subject, which was the price of onions. I started out as a genial wanderer, but I am beginning to sound like an evangelist. That will not do. So, arrivederci!

Index